W9-CZX-491

VERBIS NON FACTIS

Words Meant to Influence Political Choices in the United States, 1800-1980

by

FAY M. BLAKE
and
H. MORTON NEWMAN

The Scarecrow Press, Inc.
Metuchen, N.J., & London
1984

Library of Congress Cataloging in Publication Data

Blake, Fay M., 1920–
    Verbis non factis.

    Bibliography: p.
    Includes index.
    1. Political parties--United States--History--Miscel-
lanea. 2. Political slogans--United States. 3. Presi-
dents--United States--Election--History--Miscellanea.
4. United States--Politics and government--Miscellanea.
I. Newman, H. Morton. II. Title.
JK2261.B618 1984   324.2'3   84-1325
ISBN 0-8108-1688-1

Dedicated to the grandchildren:

Allison Newman
Cietta Penn
Nat Penn
Adam Rogers
Chris Uzdavinis

in the hope that their political activity
will outstrip ours.

ACKNOWLEDGMENTS

Our grateful thanks to Bruce Boylen for the many hours he spent dredging in the windy rhetoric of national Party platforms; to historian Marion Casey, our friend and colleague, for her fruitful suggestions and her steady encouragement; to the fine reference librarians at Berkeley Public Library and at Doe Library, University of California, Berkeley for their cheerful help.

It should be noted that all the typing of this manuscript was done by the male member of the team. The female member is most appreciative and heartily endorses the arrangement and recommends it to other couples.

CONTENTS

NOTE TO USERS

The 1,062 slogans in this book are listed chronologically. Each slogan is numbered and identified by year, political party that originated the slogan, and the presidential candidate of that party. For each slogan there is also a symbol in parentheses representing at least one citation: a book in which there is a reference to the slogan and the page on which the reference appears. For example,

When Grover Goes Marching Home. (F 72)

means the reference will be found in Beryl Frank's Pictorial History of the Democratic Party on page 72. The Key to Citations appears on page 115.

In addition to the chronological listing there are three indexes: political parties, names of people, and keywords in the slogans. Each entry in the indexes refers to the consecutively numbered slogans in the main listing.

INTRODUCTION

We came to compile this collection of political slogans by a
kind of natural process since we have behind us almost a century of combined political activity in our lives, including the
State Chairmanship of one political party and State Committee
membership in another. So both of us have been exposed to
more than an average dose of political slogans. We've long
ago discarded any belief in the truth or accuracy of slogans
--if we ever had any--but continue to be interested in them
as aspects of social history and political behavior. We hope
the book will bring back memories to browsers or help others
locate some elusive catchword from the past.

The word "slogan," we discover from the dictionary,
is from the Gaelic and meant originally an army yell, the
shouted motto by which one Highland clan identified another.
In this book we use "slogan" rather elastically to mean
phrases or short sentences or jingles which arose in the
course of a political campaign and were then repeated to
pinpoint and emphasize some aspect of the campaign--an issue, a characteristic of a candidate, a grievance, a hope or
a wish. The sources for the slogans are varied. They come
from national party platforms; from banners, placards, bumper stickers, buttons and other printed giveaways used during
political campaigns; from campaign songs; from speeches at
conventions; from newspaper cartoons; from advertisements
in journals and papers; and later on from radio talks and
commercials, and most recently from TV. We were aiming
at collecting and identifying about a thousand slogans and have
ended with a thousand and a few more for good measure cov-
ering the years 1800 to 1980. The year 1800 is a starting
point not only because it's a good round number but because

parties first became well-defined elements of American political campaigning at that time. Federalists and Republicans (not the direct ancestors of our present Republican Party) squared off and hurled accusations, insults, and dares at each other in 1800 with the same gusto and with just about the same modicum of rationality and sense as party slogans do now. The year 1980 seemed a good stopping place because it was the year of our most recent presidential campaign, and several published analyses of the events of 1980 refer to slogans generated during the course of the campaign.

Most of the slogans in this book center around American presidential campaigns, although we've tossed in a few which originated during various wars--World Wars I and II, the Mexican, Civil, Spanish-American, Korean and Vietnam Wars. We also couldn't resist a few stemming from the Depression of the 1930's, which both of us experienced personally. For each slogan we have included at least one citation from a printed source, but in a few cases we have used slogans we ourselves have seen on banners, placards, bumper stickers, or buttons in museum displays; in newsreels or documentary films; and in demonstrations and marches which we observed or in which we participated. The books we have used as citations are, for the most part, not scholarly historical studies, but the popular illustrated histories in which political slogans most often appear.

There is no apparent rule for what becomes a slogan. Some obscure issue can be picked up as a chant at a convention, and then continue to be used "again and again and again" (to quote one of the slogans we include). Whenever an elected president is running for re-election the slogan "Four more years" seems almost inevitable. Alliteration, doggerel verse, and puns are seemingly irresistible to sloganeers (cf., "Win with Willkie," "Van, Van Is a Used Up Man," "Old Tip-ler"). That "little brown brother" and "a splendid little war" became popular and were endlessly repeated after the Spanish-American War in 1898 probably reflects the widespread racism and jingoism of the American political scene as well as the brevity of both these phrases. President McKinley's much more pious cover-up for American colonialism never became a popular slogan. He said he had decided, after sincere prayer, that it was essential for the United States to annex the Philippines because we needed to "educate, uplift, civilize and Christianize the Filipinos." There's a certain swing and rhythm to the phrase and a certain comfort to those who had some qualms about the impe-

rialist venture, but it turned out not to be slogan material.
More recently, a president turned sloganeer and at least
briefly had some success with his attempt. Ronald Reagan's
persistently repeated "Stay the course" in 1982 had a vogue
for a few weeks before it was quietly mothballed. What becomes a slogan, then, is not only what is brief, easily re-
membered, and repeatable, but also what is persistently
pushed by contemporary media. The presidential campaign
of 1840 was the first to use a full panoply of hoopla and hype
with torchlight parades, buttons, advertisements, and a ple-
thora of slogans. Mostly they concentrated on Whig candidate
William Henry Harrison's heroism during the Battle of Tippecanoe in 1811, a minor skirmish which had occurred twenty-
nine years earlier. Another issue resulting in a number of
slogans during the same campaign was the simplicity of the
"ploughman" candidate, Harrison, contrasted in the aristocratic tastes of his opponent, Van Buren. The slogans failed
to note that Harrison's simple little farm was a 2,000-acre
spread and that Harrison was a rich man with many business
interests whose life had little in common with that of the dis-
tressed dirt farmers. His Democratic opponents also pro-
duced various slogans which hammered away at Harrison's
drinking habits. But the Whig slogans must have worked.
Harrison won the election.

Humor, often unconscious, frequently intrudes into
political slogans. Personal peccadillos, physical peculiarities,
and suspected weaknesses of opposition candidates often become taunting and funny slogans. William Howard Taft's
weight, Martin Van Buren's taste in French food and wine,
James Blaine's and Grover Cleveland's illegitimate children
all found their way into slogans of the time. On the other
hand, some political issues resulted in angry and bitter slogans, most recently witnessed in the opposition to the Vietnam War. The vast majority of the slogans, however, are
bland almost meaningless repetitions of abstract qualities.
Justice, Right, Truth, Wealth, the Nation, and the People's
Choice persist and continue to crop up campaign after campaign. We refrain from drawing obvious conclusions from
the fact that the single most popular word in over a thousand
slogans in almost two hundred years has been "WAR."

The mind industry can take on anything, digest
it, reproduce it, and pour it out. Whatever
our minds can conceive of is grist to its mill,
nothing will leave it unadulterated; it is capable
of turning any idea into a slogan and any work
of the imagination into a hit.

> --Hans Magnus Enzensberger, "The Indus-
> trialization of the Mind," 1962; from Raids
> and Reconstructions: Essays on Politics,
> Crime and Culture (London: Pluto Press,
> 1976).

CHRONOLOGICAL LIST OF SLOGANS

1. We are all Republicans. We are all Federalists. (LO 63)
   1800--Republican Party--Jefferson
   From Jefferson's first inaugural speech.

2. The Revolution of 1800. (LO 69)
   1800--Republican Party--Jefferson
   Jefferson's comment on his own election.

3. Sound the tocsin about Jefferson. (S 121)
   1800--Federalist Party--Adams
   A Federalist attack on Jefferson.

4. Anarchy can create more evil in a year than ... government can eradicate in a century. (S 152)
   1800--Federalist Party--Adams
   A Federalist warning against the Republicans.

5. Religious liberty, the rights of conscience, no priesthood, truth and Jefferson. (S 124)
   1800--Republican Party--Jefferson
   A version of the Republican platform from the Philadelphia Aurora.

6. God and a religious president or Jefferson and no God! (S 124)
   1800--Federalist Party--Adams
   A Federalist diatribe against Jefferson.

7. Friend of the people. (S 123)

1

1800--Republican Party--Jefferson
Slogan of Jefferson's supporters.

8. Those who labor in the earth are the chosen people of God.   (S 123)
1800--Republican Party--Jefferson
Republican campaign slogan.

9. High time for a change.   (S 121)
1800--Republican Party--Jefferson
From a Republican campaign leaflet.

10. American Cato.   (DAP 15)
1800--Federalist Party--Adams
Federalist characterization of Adams.

11. Bibles will be burned, property rights destroyed, and the marriage institution abolished.   (BO 35)
1800--Federalist Party--Adams
A Federalist attack on Jefferson because of his sympathy with the French Revolution.

12. Federalist Reign of Terror.   (B 180)
1800--Republican Party--Jefferson
Republican attack on Federalists.

13. Lord! How the Federalists will stare / At Jefferson, in Adams' chair.   (B 180)
1800--Republican Party--Jefferson
Republican prediction of victory.

14. Few die and none resign.   (DAP 155)
1804--Republican Party--Jefferson
A misquote from Jefferson who actually said (July 12, 1801) about the Civil Service: "Those by death are few, by resignation none."

15. In politics, Mr. Madison is a Frenchman.   (S 211)
1808--Federalist Party--Pinckney
Madison, successor to Jefferson, was accused by Federalists of supporting the French Revolution.

16. Oh! this cursed Ograbme.   (LOR 69)
1808--Federalist Party--Pinckney
A reference to Jefferson's unpopular embargo (spelled backward).

17. Dambargo. (LO 83)
     1808--Federalist Party--Pinckney
     Attack on Jefferson's unpopular embargo against
     trade with Great Britain.

18. Virginia Lordlings. (B 199)
     1808--Federalist Party--Pinckney
     Attack on Republican "dynasty" and its leaders from
     the Virginia aristocracy.

19. Gerrymandering. (LO 90)
     1812--Federalist Party--Clinton
     An attack by the Federalists against Elbridge Gerry,
     Republican Vice-Presidential candidate, for unfair
     senatorial redistricting in Massachusetts.

20. Vigor in war, and a determined character in peace.
     (S 257)
     1812--Federalist Party--Clinton
     Campaign slogan by Clinton supporters.

21. Peace and commerce. (S 258)
     1812--Federalist Party--Clinton
     Slogan for Clinton.

22. War Hawks. (B 202)
     1812--Republican Party--Madison
     Nickname for bloc of legislators, including Clay and
     Calhoun, pushing Madison into an aggressive stance
     against England.

23. Free trade and sailor's rights. (B 203; DAP 167)
     1812--Republican Party--Madison
     Slogan of those advocating a strong stand against
     England.

24. Mr. Madison's War. (BO 46)
     1816--Federalist Party--King
     Opponents' characterization of the War of 1812.

25. Remember the River Raisin. (DAP 324)
     1816--Republican Party--Monroe
     A reference to an incident (January 22, 1813) in
     which Indians murdered American prisoners of
     the British during the War of 1812.

26. Blue Lights. (DAP 40)

1816--Republican Party--Monroe
An attack on Federalists who were accused of warning the British of the presence of an American
fleet in New London, Connecticut during the War
of 1812.

27.   Virginia Dynasty.   (DAP 394; B 226)
1816--Federalist Party--King
An attack on the Republican leaders (Jefferson,
Madison and Monroe) as Virginia aristocrats.

28.   Era of Good Feeling.   (LO 105; BO 51)
1820--Republican Party--Monroe
A slogan reflecting the end of the War of 1812 and
a period of prosperity.

29.   Period of Personal Politics.   (DAP 287)
1820--Republican Party--Monroe
A characterization of a period in which the Federalist Party had disintegrated amid dissensions.

30.   Missouri Compromise.   (DAP 247; MO, v2, 139)
1820--Republican Party--Monroe
Admission of Missouri as a slave state, Maine as a
free state and prohibition of slavery north of lati-
tude 36° 30' since Missouri had voted in the presidential election although not yet admitted as a
state.

31.   Monroe Doctrine.   (B 240; DAP 248; MO, v2, 149)
1824--National Republican Party--J. Q. Adams
Monroe's annual message to Congress on December
2, 1823, enunciated the principle of freedom of
the American continents from future European
colonization.

32.   American System.   (LO 122; DAP 17; MO, v2, 135)
1824--National Republican Party--J. Q. Adams
Advocacy of protective tariffs to develop American
industry, named by Clay.

33.   Republican Principles.   (S 363, 395)
1824--National Republican Party--J. Q. Adams
Slogan of John Quincy Adams' supporters.

34.   A convicted adulteress and her paramour husband.
(LOR 110)

1824--Democratic Party--Jackson
An attack on Jackson and his wife, Rachel, accused
of marrying before her divorce from her first
husband was final.

35. Down with King Caucus. (B 244)
1824--Democratic Party--Jackson
An attack on the caucus system of presidential nom-
inations and for direct popular participation.

36. The People Must be Heard! (B 244)
1824--Democratic Party--Jackson
Jackson was being promoted as a "Man of the People. "

37. Science gives peace and America plenty. (D 12)
1824--National Republican Party--J. Q. Adams
A reflection of the beginnings of American techno-
logical development.

38. The glorious principles of seventy-six. (S 367, 399)
1824--Democratic Party--Jackson
Jackson's supporters claimed him as representative
of the spirit of the American Revolution.

39. Adams and Clay Republicans. (DAP 3)
1828--National Republican Party--J. Q. Adams
By 1825 the Republican Party was splitting into
various factions, one of which supported John
Quincy Adams in the 1828 elections.

40. Shall the people rule? (B 252)
1828--Democratic Party--Jackson
Jackson's supporters emphasized his "people's"
candidacy.

41. Huzza for Jackson! Down with the Yankees! (B 252)
1828--Democratic Party--Jackson
A Southern campaign poster.

42. Bloody Deeds of General Jackson. (LOR 105; S 485)
1828--National Republican Party--J. Q. Adams
The notorious "Coffin Handbill" accused Jackson of
ordering the execution of six militiamen during
the War of 1812.

43. Corrupt bargain. (S 414; BO 59)

      1828--Democratic Party--Jackson
      Jackson's supporters accused Adams of a deal with
        Clay repaying election help by appointing Clay
        his Secretary of State.

44. Middle and just course. (S 419)
      1828--Democratic Party--Jackson
      Jackson would support moderate protectionist tariffs.

45. Jackson and reform. (S 432)
      1828--Democratic Party--Jackson

46. The people or the aristocracy. (LOR 106)
      1828--Democratic Party--Jackson
      Jackson's supporters proposed him as the antidote
        to the aristocratic opposition.

47. Save the Temple of Liberty from pollution. (S 474)
      1828--National Republican Party--J. Q. Adams
      Jackson would destroy moderation and culture,
        opponents claimed.

48. Jackson, Calhoun and Liberty. (S 433)
      1828--Democratic Party--Jackson
      Calhoun ran as Vice-Presidential candidate with
        Jackson.

49. Friends of peace! Lovers of liberty! Preserve your
    country! (S 481)
      1828--National Republican Party--J. Q. Adams

50. All Hail Old Hickory. (B 252)
      1828--Democratic Party--Jackson

51. Old Hickory. (BO 67)
      1828--Democratic Party--Jackson
      The nickname given Jackson by the press.

52. The hero of New Orleans. (S 416)
      1828--Democratic Party--Jackson
      Jackson led 5,000 Americans to victory over the
        British on January 8, 1815, with the loss of only
        13 men to 2,000 British casualties.

53. The Farmer of Tennessee. (BO 67)
      1828--Democratic Party--Jackson
      Jackson pictured as down-to-earth man of the people.

54. Democracy Prevails Throughout the Nation. (CCB 16)
     1828--Democratic Party--Jackson
     Jackson as the candidate for democracy and the
        "common people" (John Adams' phrase).

55. The Advocate of the American System. (CCB 15)
     1828--Democratic Party--Jackson
     (See entry no. 32.)

56. People's candidate. (LO 124; S 419)
     1828--Democratic Party--Jackson
     Jackson was put forward as the more democratic
        and popular candidate.

57. King Mob. (LO 126)
     1828--National Republican Party--J. Q. Adams
     Jackson's opponents pictured him as ruled by "the
        mob."

58. Hickory pole canvass. (DAP 185)
     1828--Democratic Party--Jackson
     The Democratic Party emblem was a hickory pole
        for candidate Andrew Jackson, nicknamed Old
        Hickory.

59. Tariff of Abominations. (DAP 1)
     1832--Democratic Party--Jackson
     South Carolina nullified the Tariff in 1828. Jackson
        swore to use Federal troops, if necessary, to
        enforce the law.

60. November, November--the second's the hour! (LOR
     126)
     1832--National Republican Party--Clay
     A plea to get out the vote for Clay.

61. Our federal union, it must be preserved. (LO 135;
     B 266; DAP 276)
     1832--Democratic Party--Jackson
     A toast by Jackson on April 13, 1830.

62. The Union, Next to Our Liberty, Most Dear! (B 261)
     1832--National Republican Party--Clay
     A toast by Calhoun in response to Jackson (see
        entry no. 61) on April 13, 1830.

63. Freedom and Clay. (B 267)
     1832--National Republican Party--Clay

64. Annexationist. (DAP 19)
    1832--Democratic Party--Jackson
    A wing of the Jacksonians who advocated expansion
    of U.S. territory by annexation of Texas.

65. To the victors belong the spoils. (LOR 117; LO 129;
    S 938)
    1832--Democratic Party--Jackson
    Jackson's policy of replacing civil servants by his
    own supporters was justified by New York Demo-
    crat William I. Marcy in this phrase.

66. Downfall of Mother Bank. (LO 143)
    1832--Democratic Party--Jackson
    Jackson consistently opposed the Bank of the United
    States (see entry no. 72).

67. Despotism--Anarchy--Disunion. (LOR 127)
    1832--National Republican Party--Clay
    A South Carolina convention declared Tariff of
    Abominations null and void and accused Jackson
    of spreading dissension. Clay devised a compro-
    mise tariff.

68. Nullification! (LO 134)
    1832--National Republican Party--Clay
    Opposition to the "Tariff of Abominations" (which
    Jackson vowed to uphold) resulted in demands
    for nullification of the tariff.

69. "THE KING UPON THE THRONE: The people in the
    Dust! ! !" (S 511)
    1832--National Republican Party--Clay
    Jackson was pictured as a despot.

70. King Andrew the First. (LO 137)
    1832--National Republican Party--Clay
    Cartoons, pamphlets and editorials characterized
    Jackson as an absolute ruler.

71. Eaton Malaria. (LO 130)
    1832--National Republican Party--Clay
    Jackson was attacked for championing Peggy O'Neale
    Eaton, wife of his Secretary of War, who was
    snubbed by Washington society.

72. The Bank Must Perish: The Union Must and Shall Be

Preserved. (CCB 19)
1832--Democratic Party--Jackson
Jackson's opposition to the Bank of the United States
(see entry no. 66).

73. The Champion of Republicanism and the American System. (CCB 21)
1832--National Republican Party--Clay
Clay's protectionist advocacy (see entry no. 32).

74. Albany Regency. (LO 130; DAP 12)
1832--National Republican Party--Clay
An attack on Jackson's support among New York
Democrats, including his Vice-Presidential candidate, Martin Van Buren.

75. He stands by the People. (S 509)
1832--Democratic Party--Jackson

76. Jackson Forever: Go the Whole Hog. (B 267)
1832--Democratic Party--Jackson

77. Emperor Nick of the Bribery Bank. (B 266; LOR 131)
1832--Democratic Party--Jackson
A reference to Nicholas Biddle, aristocratic president of the Bank of the United States.

78. Perish Credit. Perish Commerce. Down with the Bank. (CCB 24)
1832--Democratic Party--Jackson
From a campaign button of 1832.

79. Non-committalism. (BO 86, 88)
1836--Whig Party--William H. Harrison
Whigs accused Democratic candidate Van Buren of a
customary failure to take strong and principled
stands.

80. Compromise tariff. (DAP 82)
1836--Whig Party--William H. Harrison
The Whigs took credit for Clay's compromise proposal (1833) to satisfy both protectionists (Whigs)
and free traders (Democrats).

81. The principles and prudence of our forefathers who can
justly appreciate liberty and equality. (CCB 29)
1836--Democratic Party--Van Buren
From a Van Buren campaign button.

82. Federalists, nullifiers and bank men. (S 578)
    1836--Democratic Party--Van Buren
    Democrats' characterization of the Whigs.

83. Union, harmony, self-denial, concession, everything
    for the cause, nothing for men. (S 585)
    1836--Democratic Party--Van Buren
    Campaign slogan devised at a meeting of Democratic
    Congressmen.

84. Our country, not our Party. (S 586)
    1836--Whig Party--William H. Harrison

85. Firm Friend of the South. (S 590)
    1836--Democratic Party--Van Buren

86. Remember the Alamo! (DAP 324; MO, v2, 314)
    1836--Democratic Party--Van Buren
    Sam Houston's cavalry rode into battle on April 21,
    1836, shouting this slogan and defeated Mexican
    General Santa Anna.

87. Locofocos. (LO 147)
    1836--Democratic Party--Van Buren
    Radical New York Democrats calling themselves the
    Equal Rights Party but nicknamed "locofocos"
    (matches) when they met in rump session and
    used candles to light the darkened hall.

88. Little Magician. (DU 71)
    1836--Democratic Party--Van Buren
    Van Buren was short and had a reputation as a
    clever manipulator.

89. Red Fox of Kinderhook. (DU 71)
    1836--Democratic Party--Van Buren
    Another nickname for Van Buren who had a home at
    Kinderhook in upstate New York.

90. American Talleyrand. (DU 71)
    1836--Democratic Party--Van Buren
    Another nickname for the shrewd Van Buren.

91. Equal and full protection to American Industry. (CCB
    30)
    1836--Whig Party--William H. Harrison
    Clay, originator of this slogan, agreed with Whig

protectionist policies although he was the author
of the Compromise Tariff (see entry no. 80).

92. Democracy and our Country. (CCB 28)
    1836--Democratic Party--Van Buren
    A play on the name of the emerging Democratic
    Party; from a Van Buren campaign button.

93. The Kinderhook Poney and the Ohio Ploughman. (LO
    141)
    1836--Democratic Party--Van Buren
        Whig Party--Harrison
    Van Buren is the Kinderhook Poney and Harrison
    the Ohio ploughman.

94. "Dandy" Van Buren. (LO 146)
    1836--Whig Party--Harrison
    A Whig allusion to Van Buren's dapper appearance
    and expensive habits.

95. Bread, Meat, Rent and Fuel! / Their prices must
    come down! (Z 219)
    1836--Democratic Party--Van Buren
    A slogan of the Locofocos (Equal Rights Party), a
    radical wing of the Democrats.

96. Millions for Defence, Not One Cent for Tribute!
    (CCB 34)
    1840--Whig Party--Harrison
    The phrase actually dates back to 1798, but was
    used on a Whig campaign button in 1840.

97. Log cabin and hard cider candidate. (LO 158)
    1840--Whig Party--Harrison
    Originally a Democratic taunt, the Whigs took the
        phrase describing Harrison's humble origins
        and drinking preference as their campaign slo-
        gan.

98. Another gourd for General Mum / Whose fame is like
    his favorite drum; / Which when most empty makes
    most noise / Huzza for General Mum, my boys.
    (S 672; BO 91)
        1840--Democrats--Van Buren
        Democratic attack on Harrison; "General Mum"
        because he evaded issues.

99. Farmer of North Bend.   (BO 90)
     1840--Whig Party--Harrison

100. Matty's policy, $12\frac{1}{2}$ cents a day and French soup; our
     policy, 2 dollars a day and Roast Beef.   (S 673)
     1840--Whig Party--Harrison
     A Whig attack on Van Buren and the Democrats.

101. Van's popularity fills the great West; / His firmness and
     honesty none can contest.   (S 672)
     1840--Democratic Party--Van Buren

102. Hush a-bye-baby Daddy's a Whig / Before he comes
     home Hard cider he'll swig; / Then he'll be tipsy and
     over he'll fall; / Down will come Daddy, Tip, Tyler
     and all.   (S 672)
     1840-- Democratic Party--Van Buren
     Democrats attacked Harrison as a heavy drinker.

103. "Old Tip-ler."   (S 671; BO 90)
     1840--Democratic Party--Van Buren
     Another Democratic reference to Harrison's sup-
     posed drinking habits.

104. Federalism and Abolition United.   (S 671)
     1840--Democratic Party--Van Buren
     Democratic characterization of the Whigs.

105. Hurrah and Hallelujah Campaign.   (S 948)
     1840--Democratic Party--Van Buren
     Democratic Party attack on Whig campaign tactics.

106. The battle is now between the log cabin and the pal-
     aces, between hard cider and champagne.   (LOR 151)
     1840--Whig Party--Harrison
     Clay's slogan putting Whig democratic roots against
     Democrats' aristocratic tendencies.

107. Steam Boat Van Buren for Salt River Direct Loco-
     Foco Line.   (CCB 50)
     1840--Whig Party--Harrison
     A Whig campaign button attacking Van Buren as
     following the radical Democrat (Locofoco) line.

108. Harrison and Reform, the Hero of Tippecanoe.   (CCB
     55)
     1840--Whig Party--Harrison

Harrison defeated Tecumseh and a small party of Indians in the "Battle of Tippecanoe" on November 7, 1811, slogan from an election poster.

109. Harrison; Two Dollars a Day and Roast Beef.   (B 278)
1840--Whig Party--Harrison

110. Ole Tip, he wears a homespun shirt, / He has no ruffled shirt, wirt, wirt / But Matt, he has the golden plate / And he's a little squirt, wirt, wirt.   (B 278; BO 91)
1840--Whig Party--Harrison
Harrison the "man of the people" vs. Van Buren the "aristocrat."

111. Let Van from his coolers of silver drink wine / And lounge on his cushioned settee / Our man on his buckeye bench can recline / Content with hard cider is he. (PO 123)
1840--Whig Party--Harrison

112. Old Kinderhook.   (LO 165)
1840--Democratic Party--Van Buren
A reference to Van Buren's birthplace in upstate New York.   The initials are claimed to be the origin of "O. K. " meaning approval.

113. Keep the ball rolling.   (LO 165)
1840--Whig Party--Harrison
A reference to a huge ball with Whig campaign slogans rolled through the streets of Baltimore during a campaign parade.

114. A man in an iron cage.   (LO 161)
1840--Democratic Party--Van Buren
The Democrats' slogan attacking Harrison as the puppet of his campaign committee.

115. With Tip and Tyler / We'll bust Van's biler.   (LO 155)
1840--Whig Party--Harrison

116. Rumpsey-dumpsey, rumpsey-dumpsey / Colonel Johnson killed Tecumseh.   (MO, v2, 198; LO 152)
1840--Democratic Party--Van Buren
Richard Johnson, Van Buren's running mate, claimed to have killed Tecumseh at the Battle of the Thames.

117. You can't come it, Marty. (CCB 63)
     1840--Whig Party--Harrison
     A taunt against Van Buren.

118. The firm and fearless advocate of democracy. (CCB
     61)
          1840--Democratic Party--Van Buren
          Democrats' characterization of Van Buren on a
          campaign button.

119. The people's money safe bind, safe find. (CCB 60)
     1840--Democratic Party--Van Buren
     Van Buren's supporters tried to defend him from
          the charge that his and Jackson's fiscal policies
          had caused the severe depression of 1837.

120. The Advocate of equal rights. (CCB 60)
     1840--Democratic Party--Van Buren
     Van Buren was accused of aristocratic tastes and
          elitist policy by his opponents.

121. A uniform and sound currency. (CCB 60)
     1840--Democratic Party--Van Buren
     From a campaign button defending Van Buren from
          charges of unsound monetary policies.

122. Martin Van Buren and Democracy, / Our principles
     are justice and equality. (CCB 59)
          1840--Democratic Party--Van Buren
          Another campaign button.

123. Weighed in the balance and found wanting. (CCB 51)
     1840--Whig Party--Harrison
     A Whig button attacking the Democrats.

124. Farewell, dear Van / You are not our man / To
     guide the ship / We'll try Old Tip. (S 643; LO 158)
          1840--Whig Party--Harrison
          "Tip" from Tippecanoe, Harrison's nickname.

125. Tippecanoe and Tyler, too! (BO 90; S 643; LO 152)
     1840--Whig Party--Harrison
     Harrison campaigned with his Vice-Presidential
          candidate, John Tyler, as the hero of the Battle
          of Tippecanoe in 1811.

126. Without a why or wherefore / We'll go for Harrison

therefore.   (S 673)
  1840--Whig Party--Harrison

127. Make way for old Tip, turn out, turn out! / 'Tis the people's decree / Their choice shall he be / So Martin Van Buren turn out, turn out!   (S 680; LO 159)
  1840--Whig Party--Harrison

128. Union and Harmony.   (LOR 153)
  1840--Whig Party--Harrison
    A reference to Clay's withdrawal as Whig candidate at the convention with the phrase: "If my name creates any obstacles to union and harmony."

129. The people are coming.   (S 669)
  1840--Whig Party--Harrison
    Harrison and the Whigs campaigned as representatives of the "common man."

130. No Reduction in Wages.   (S 669)
  1840--Whig Party--Harrison
    Van Buren was blamed for the wage reductions in the 1837 depression.

131. Van, Van, Van, / Van is a used-up man.   (S 643)
  1840--Whig Party--Harrison
    A Whig attack on Van Buren.

132. Honor Where Honor's Due ... To the Hero of Tippecanoe.   (CCB 39)
  1840--Whig Party--Harrison
    A campaign button.

133. The People's Choice....   The Hero of Tippecanoe.   (CCB 40)
  1840--Whig Party--Harrison
    A campaign button.

134. The Log Cabin Candidate....   The People's Choice.   (CCB 45)
  1840--Whig Party--Harrison

135. He leaves the plough to save his country.   (CCB 46)
  1840--Whig Party--Harrison
    Harrison's rich 2,000-acre farm in North Bend, Ohio became, for campaign purposes, a poor farm where Harrison "ploughs his own ground."

136. Go It Tip, Come It Tyler. (CCB 47)
     1840--Whig Party--Harrison
     A campaign button for Harrison and Tyler.

137. Am I Not a Woman & a Sister / Am I Not a Man & a
     Brother. (CCB 36)
     1840--Abolitionist Party--James G. Birney
     A rare third-party campaign button opposing slav-
     ery.

138. Law and order. (LOR 176)
     1844--Whig Party--Clay
     From a Whig parade banner.

139. Who Is Polk? (BO 99; S 784)
     1844--Whig Party--Clay
     Asked sarcastically by Clay when Polk became the
     nominee, then picked up as a Whig slogan.

140. Polk, Slavery and Texas, or Clay, Union and Liberty.
     (S 789; B 289)
     1844--Whig Party--Clay
     Clay opposed the annexation of Texas and the ex-
     pansion of slavery.

141. Oregon fever. (B 288)
     1844--Democratic Party--Polk
     Democrats supported expansion into Oregon.

142. Redeem the country, restore prosperity. (LOR 177)
     1844--Whig Party--Clay

143. Hooray for Clay. (LOR 177)
     1844--Whig Party--Clay

144. Reannexation of Texas and reoccupation of Oregon.
     (LOR 173)
     1844--Democratic Party--Polk
     Expansionist policies were in the Democratic Party
     platform of 1844.

145. Press Onward--Enlarge the Boundaries of Freedom,
     Young Hickory--Equal Protection to All Classes.
     (CCB 66)
     1844--Democratic Party--Polk
     A Democratic campaign button stressing expansion-
     ism and Polk as successor to Jackson, "Old
     Hickory."

146. A Tariff for Protection. (CCB 79)
        1844--Whig Party--Clay
        The Whigs supported a protectionist tariff.

147. United We Stand, Divided We Fall. (CCB 69)
        1844--Democratic Party--Polk
        This slogan appeared on a campaign button for
            George Dallas, the Vice-Presidential candidate,
            but was widely used in later campaigns as well.

148. Our Country Right or Wrong. (CCB 69)
        1844--Democratic Party--Polk
        From a contemporary campaign button.

149. Polk, Dallas, Texas and Democracy. (LO 182)
        1844--Democratic Party--Polk
        A Democratic slogan for Polk and his running
            mate, Dallas, stressing expansion of the United
            States into Texas.

150. All Oregon or none. (LO 182)
        1844--Democratic Party--Polk
        The Democrats advocated annexation of both Texas
            and Oregon.

151. All of Texas, All of Oregon. (LO 180)
        1844--Democratic Party--Polk

152. Young Hickory. (S 785; LO 177)
        1844--Democratic Party--Polk
        A reference to Polk as the successor of Jackson,
            "Old Hickory."

153. Union, Harmony and Vigilance. (F 24)
        1844--Democratic Party--Polk
        From a "National Badge," a campaign leaflet of
            the day.

154. Clay and Frelinghuysen--Protection and Union. (CCB
        84)
        1844--Whig Party--Clay
        Frelinghuysen was Clay's running mate.

155. A halo shines as bright as day / Around the head of
        Henry Clay. (CCB 77)
        1844--Whig Party--Clay
        Well, maybe.

156. Let us encourage our own manufactures. (CCB 76)
     1844--Whig Party--Clay
     The Whigs advocated high protective tariffs and the
     development of United States industry.

157. Our flag tramped upon. Natives, / Beware of Foreign
     Influence. (CCB 72-3)
     1844--Native American Party--Clay
     The Native American Party were vociferously xeno-
     phobic and endorsed Clay; this slogan from a
     campaign button.

158. The wealth of a nation is indicated by its industry.
     (CCB 71)
     1844--Whig Party--Clay
     Whigs emphasized American industrial development.

159. The flag we wear at our masthead should be the cre-
     dentials of our seamen. (CCB 71)
     1844--Whig Party--Clay
     Although Clay opposed annexation of territory, the
     Whigs strongly advocated United States national-
     ism.

160. Napoleon of the stump. (BO 100)
     1844--Democratic Party--Polk
     Democrats referred affectionately to Polk's short
     stature and forensic skill.

161. Henry Clay and Protection to All our Enterprises.
     (CCB 70)
     1844--Whig Party--Clay
     Campaign button.

162. Henry Clay, the Champion of a Protective Tariff.
     (CCB 69)
     1844--Whig Party--Clay
     Campaign button.

163. Fifty-four forty or fight! (LO 182; DAP 156)
     1844--Democratic Party--Polk
     Annexationists demanded the boundary line for Ore-
     gon be drawn at latitude 54° 40'.

164. Corporal's Guard. (DAP 99)
     1844--Tyler
     The nickname for disaffected Whigs and Democrats

who briefly supported Tyler for President until Tyler withdrew from the race.

165. Human brotherhood, true Democracy, pure Christianity. (J 4)
   1844--Liberty Party (Abolitionists)--James Birney
   From the platform of this small third party which opposed slavery.

166. For Liberty, not for Despotism.   (J 8)
   1844--Liberty Party--Birney
   From the party's platform.

167. Liberty and Union Now and Forever One and Inseparable.   (CCB 78)
   1844--Whig Party--Clay
   From a campaign button.

168. The name of Henry Clay needs no eulogy.   (J 9)
   1844--Whig Party--Clay
   From the Whig platform.

169. Texas or Disunion.   (B 286)
   1844--Tyler
   A few Whigs and Democrats supported Tyler against both Democrat Polk and Whig Clay, but Tyler withdrew when he failed to gain a substantial following.

170. Auspicium Melioris Avei.   (CCB 77)
   1844--Whig Party--Clay
   When politicians still took pride in a classical education, from a Clay campaign button.

171. Protection to the working class is an assurance of success.   (CCB 77)
   1844--Whig Party--Clay
   Part of the Whig's advocacy of United States industrial development--memorialized on a campaign button.

172. Non sibi sed patriae.   (CCB 77)
   1844--Whig Party--Clay
   See also entry no. 84 for another version in English.

173. Clay, Union, and Liberty.   (S 789)
   1844--Whig Party--Clay

174. The Abolition Candidate of the North. (S 788)
     1844--Whig Party--Clay
     Early shadows of coming events. The Abolition
     Party was running its own candidate, Birney,
     in the 1844 election.

175. Manifest Destiny. (Z 149; DAP 237; BO 100; LO 185;
     B 280; M 15)
     1848--Democratic Party--Cass
     After the war with Mexico in 1846, Democrats
     fervently advocated expansion. This popular
     phrase came from John O'Sullivan, editor of
     the Democratic Review, who wrote in 1845:
     "Our manifest destiny to overspread the conti-
     nent allotted by Providence for the free develop-
     ment of our yearly multiplying millions."

176. Ho for the Halls of Montezuma. (B 294)
     1848--Democratic Party--Cass
     A reference to the War with Mexico in 1846.

177. Mexico or Death. (B 294; Z 158)
     1848--Democratic Party--Cass
     Another Mexican War slogan.

178. American blood on the American soil. (LOR 181;
     B 294)
     1848--Democratic Party--Cass
     In the debate on the war in Mexico in 1848 Whig
     Congressman Abraham Lincoln asked on which
     "particular spot" American blood had been shed.
     Democrats asserted Mexicans had crossed the
     Rio Grande and invaded American soil.

179. Bear Flag Battalion. (DAP 35)
     1848--Democratic Party--Cass
     Expansionist sentiment erupted in California as
     well as in Oregon and Texas and in 1845 a
     California group, carrying the Bear Flag, ex-
     pelled the Mexican authorities and set up a
     provisional government.

180. Hunkers. (DAP 190; LOR 185)
     1848--Democratic Party--Cass
     The conservative wing of the New York Democrats
     who supported slavery.

181. Barnburners. (DAP 34; S 870; LOR 180)
      1848--Democratic Party--Cass
      The radical wing of the New York Democratic
          Party who opposed slavery. They supported
          Van Buren instead of the Democratic candidate
          Cass in the elections.

182. Conscience Whigs. (LOR 183; DAP 89)
      1848--Whig Party--Taylor
      The Whigs who opposed slavery.

183. Cotton Whigs. (DAP 100; LOR 183)
      1848--Whig Party--Taylor
      The Southern faction of the Whigs who were pro-
          slavery.

184. Old Hunkers. (S 870)
      1848--Whig Party--Taylor
      Whigs accused the Democratic candidate, Lewis
          Cass, of "hunkering" for political plums.

185. Untrammeled with party obligation. (LOR 183; CCB
      88)
      1848--Whig Party--Taylor
      Taylor had never even voted before 1848 so was
          unidentified with political partisanship. He de-
          clared, "If elected, I should feel bound to ad-
          minister the government untrammelled by party
          schemes."

186. Rough and Ready never surrenders. (CCB 96)
      1848--Whig Party--Taylor
      General Zachary Taylor was characterized as a
          no-nonsense military hero.

187. Liberty, Equality and Fraternity, the Cardinal Prin-
      ciples of True Democracy. (CCB 101)
      1848--Democratic Party--Cass
      A Democratic campaign button.

188. The Constitution and the Freedom of the Seas. (CCB
      102)
      1848--Democratic Party--Cass
      A campaign button of the period.

189. I would rather be right than president. (CCB 103)

1848--Whig Party--Taylor
Henry Clay insisted on a strong antislavery policy
and was, therefore, passed over as party nomi-
nee. From a campaign button.

190. Free Soil, Free Speech, Free Labor, and Free Men.
(LO 194; J 14; S 905; CCB 104)
1848--Free Soil Party--Van Buren
The slogan of the new third party opposing slavery.
Van Buren's candidacy split the Democratic vote.

191. Peace, Prosperity, and Union. (J 14)
1848--Whig Party--Taylor
From the 1848 Whig platform.

192. Old Rough and Ready. (B 295; BO 103; S 868)
1848--Whig Party--Taylor
An affectionate nickname for Zachary Taylor.

193. Economical, comical old Zach. (S 884)
1848--Democratic Party--Cass
Democrats ridiculed Whig candidate Taylor for his
stinginess. Taylor refused to accept any mail
which wasn't prepaid.

194. The Subtreasury and the tariff of Forty-Six. (CCB
101)
1848--Democratic Party--Cass
Cass was expected to adhere to the fiscal policies
of Democratic President Polk, who supported
Van Buren's proposal for subtreasuries in various cities.

195. Indemnity for the past and security for the future.
(J 18)
1852--Democratic Party--Pierce
A reference to indemnities after the Mexican War.
From the party platform.

196. The hero of many a well-fought bottle. (LOR 208)
1852--Whig Party--Scott
An allusion to Whig accusations that Pierce was a
drunkard.

197. Compromise of 1850. (DAP 82; MO, v2, 336)
1852--Whig Party--Scott
Henry Clay devised the Compromise on admission

of free and slave states, and election campaigns from 1852 to 1860 used the Compromise for campaign slogans.

198. Young Hickory of the Granite Hills. (BO 114; S 946, 1009)
    1852--Democratic Party--Pierce
    Pierce became another Young Hickory, successor to Andrew Jackson (see entry no. 153).

199. The Fainting General. (BO 114)
    1852--Whig Party--Scott
    The Whig's contemptuous nickname for Franklin Pierce, whose military record was far less illustrious than Scott's. Pierce fainted during a battle in the Mexican War.

200. Old Fuss and Feathers. (S 868; LO 211)
    1852--Democratic Party--Pierce
    The Democrats' nickname for Winfield Scott, who was regarded as vain and pompous.

201. We're bound to give the Whigs defeat / With gallant Pierce and King. (LO 210)
    1852--Democratic Party--Pierce
    A campaign song. William King was Pierce's running mate.

202. The Union and the Compromise. (LO 209)
    1852--Democratic Party--Pierce
    A reference to Clay's Compromise of 1850 (see entry no. 197).

203. Gen. Winfield Scott First in War--First in Peace. (CCB 111)
    1852--Whig Party--Scott
    An attempt to boost Scott as a worthy successor of Washington.

204. Young America. (S 1008; LO 204)
    1852--Democratic Party--Pierce
    Pierce was only 48 in 1852.

205. Concord Cabal. (S 999)
    1852--Whig Party--Scott
    The Whigs accused Pierce of listening too closely to his personal friends. Pierce was born in Concord, New Hampshire.

206. Stick of Candy Pierce. (BO 114)
    1852--Whig Party--Scott
    Whigs satirized Pierce's "reckless liberality" with
      a story about giving a little boy a stick of candy.

207. Right against wrong, and freedom against slavery.
(J 19)
    1852--Free Soil Party--Hale
    Sen. John Parker Hale, candidate of the Free Soil
      Party, was an ardent opponent of slavery.
    From the Free Soil Party Platform.

208. We Polked 'em in '44; We'll Pierce 'em in '52. (B
385)
    1852--Democratic Party--Pierce
    A punster hard at work.

209. Squatter Sovereignty. (DAP 355)
    1856--Democratic Party--Buchanan
    Democrats supported the right of settlers in
      United States territory to organize a government
      allowing slavery if they wished.

210. Free soil, free speech and Fremont. (LO 225)
    1856--Republican Party--Fremont
    The new party campaigning on an antislavery plat-
      form. A new version of a Free Soil Party slo-
      gan (see entry no. 190).

211. Americans shall (or must) rule America. (S 1020;
LO 224; DAP 15; CCB 124; J 22; B 399)
    1856--Native American Party ("Know Nothings")--
      Fillmore
    Fillmore ran on both the xenophobic Native Ameri-
      can Party and the Whig tickets.

212. The Champion of Freedom. (LO 218)
    1856--Republican Party--Fremont

213. I know nothing. (LO 223)
    1856--Native American Party ("Know Nothings")--
      Fillmore
    Native Americanists, when asked about their be-
      liefs, were supposed to answer, "I know noth-
      ing." Fillmore was their candidate, but he did
      not endorse their policies.

214. Asylum of the oppressed of every nation. (DAP 28)
     1856--Democratic Party--Buchanan
     From the party platform.

215. The Union now, the Union forever. (CCB 124)
     1856--Whig Party--Fillmore

216. Beecher's Bibles. (LOR 218)
     1856--Republican Party--Fremont
     Nickname for rifles sent to Kansas settlers by
     New England abolitionists.

217. Free Kansas and the Union. (CCB 119)
     1856--Republican Party--Fremont
     A reference to the increasingly violent slavery dis-
     putes in Kansas.

218. Bleeding Kansas. (B 398; S 1018)
     1856--Republican Party--Fremont
     Another reference to the violence in Kansas (see
     entry nos. 216 and 219).

219. Pottawatomie Massacre. (MO, v2, 360)
     1856--Republican Party--Fremont
     A reference to John Brown's raid on a Kansas
     proslavery settlement.

220. Dark and Bloody Ground. (DAP 109)
     1856--Republican Party--Fremont
     A reference to the Kansas struggles (see entry
     nos. 216, 219, 227).

221. Crime against Kansas. (MO, v2, 361; DAP 105)
     1856--Republican Party--Fremont
     From a speech by Sen. Charles Sumner in May
     1856.

222. No North No South But the Whole Country. (CCB 122)
     1856--Whig Party--Fillmore
     An attempt to ignore the growing antislavery cam-
     paign.

223. The Rocky Mountains Echo Back Fremont, the Peo-
     ple's Choice for 1856. (CCB 117)
     1856--Republican Party--Fremont
     Fremont was the first national candidate from the
     Far West.

224. The Union one and indivisible / The crisis demands
his Election. (CCB 115)
    1856--Democratic Party--Buchanan
    The crisis was the growing struggle over slavery.

225. The Union must and shall be preserved. (CCB 113)
    1856--Democratic Party--Buchanan
    A revival of a slogan used in support of Jackson
    (see entry no. 61).

226. Free speech, free labor and eternal progression.
(CCB 118, 137)
    1856--Republican Party--Fremont
    An evolution from Free Soil Party slogans (see
    entry no. 190).

227. The Federal Constitution, the Rights of the States,
must and shall be preserved. (S 1069)
    1856--Republican Party--Fremont
    From the party platform.

228. The Union is in danger. (S 1028)
    1856--Democratic Party--Buchanan
    It certainly was.

229. We follow the Pathfinder. (S 1026; B 400)
    1856--Republican Party--Fremont
    Fremont's nickname was "The Pathfinder."

230. Woolly Heads. (S 1013)
    1856--Whig Party--Fillmore
    A racist nickname for the antislavery Whig faction
    led by William Seward.

231. Silver Greys. (S 1013)
    1856--Whig Party--Fillmore
    A nickname for the proslavery Whig faction.

232. The Nebraska Infamy. (S 1010)
    1856--Republican Party--Fremont
    The Republicans denounced the Kansas-Nebraska
    Act (1954) replacing the Missouri Compromise.

233. Conservation of the Union. (J 25)
    1856--Democratic Party--Buchanan
    From the party platform.

234. Be vigilant and watchful that internal dissensions destroy not your property. (CCB 123, 137, 234)
  1856--Whig Party--Fillmore
  From several campaign buttons. Used again in 1860 and again in 1864.

235. We are Buck Hunting. (B 400)
  1856--Republican Party--Fremont
  "Buck" for the Democratic Candidate, James Buchanan.

236. The rail-splitting candidate. (LO 241)
  1860--Republican Party--Lincoln

237. The Buchaneers. (LOR 237)
  1860--Southern Democratic Party--Breckinridge
  Led by Jefferson Davis and John Slidell, the Southern Democrats asked for Congressional protection of slavery in the territories and withdrew from the Democratic Party convention.

238. A House Divided Against Itself Cannot Stand. (DU 120)
  1860--Republican Party--Lincoln
  From the Lincoln-Douglas debates of 1858.

239. The Constitution of the country, the union of the States, and the enforcement of the laws. (S 1127; J 30; LOR 246)
  1860--Constitutional Union Party--Bell
  From the party platform.

240. The Union and the Constitution. (CCB 417)
  1860--Republican Party--Lincoln

241. Honest Old Abe. (BO 127)
  1860--Republican Party--Lincoln
  Used again in 1864.

242. What God Hath Joined Let No Man Put Asunder. (B 424)
  1860--Republican Party--Lincoln

243. Union Forever. (B 424)
  1860--Republican Party--Lincoln
  A slogan reflecting the fear that the Union would soon be split.

244. For Our Altars and Our Firesides. (B 421)
     1860--Southern Democratic Party--Breckinridge

245. Death before Dishonor. (B 421)
     1860--Southern Democratic Party--Breckinridge

246. Irrepressible conflict. (S 1111; LO 235)
     1860--Republican Party--Lincoln
     The recognition that the Civil War had become
       inevitable.

247. Union forever--freedom to all. (CCB 180)
     1860--Constitutional Union Party--Bell
     From a campaign button.

248. Our country and our rights. (CCB 190)
     1860--Southern Democratic Party--Breckinridge
     Campaign button.

249. No more slave territory. (CCB 141)
     1860--Republican Party--Lincoln
     Campaign button.

250. Millions for freedom, not one cent for slavery. (CCB
     148)
     1860--Republican Party--Lincoln
     Campaign button.

251. Vox populi, vox dei. The voice of the people is the
     voice of God. Let it be heard. (CCB 166)
     1860--Democratic Party--Douglas

252. Support "The Little Giant" Who Has Proved Himself
     the Greatest Statesman of the Age. (CCB 166)
     1860--Democratic Party--Douglas
     Douglas, like Van Buren and Polk before him, was
       short in stature.

253. The Champion of Popular Sovereignty. (CCB 167)
     1860--Democratic Party--Douglas
     Douglas was holding together the Western and
       Northern remnants of the shattered Democratic
       Party.

254. Let liberty be national and slavery sectional. (CCB
     141)
     1860--Republican Party--Lincoln
     From a campaign button.

255. Free territory for a free people. (CCB 141)
     1860--Republican Party--Lincoln
     Campaign button.

256. The man that can split rails or guide the ship of state.
     (CCB 139)
     1860--Republican Party--Lincoln
     Campaign button.

257. Freedom and protection, Lincoln & Hamlin. (CCB
     139)
     1860--Republican Party--Lincoln
     Sen. Hannibal Hamlin, a former Democrat, was
     Lincoln's running mate.

258. The fall of Sumter will be avenged, the rebellion
     crushed and the honor and integrity of the United
     States shall be maintained. (CCB 138)
     1860--Republican Party--Lincoln
     From a campaign button. Used again in 1864.

259. We will not interfere with the constitutional rights of
     any state. (CCB 138)
     1860--Republican Party--Lincoln
     Not at all the way Southern Democrats saw the
     issue. Used again in 1864.

260. The right man in the right place. (CCB 138)
     1860--Republican Party--Lincoln
     Used again in 1864.

261. The Great Rail Splitter of the West Must and Shall be
     our next President. (CCB 135)
     1860--Republican Party--Lincoln
     The "West" was Illinois.

262. Let the erring sisters go in peace. (S 1314)
     1860--Republican Party--Lincoln
     A quote from Horace Greeley, editor of the New
     York Tribune, and an influential supporter of
     Lincoln.

263. Wide Awakes. (S 1116; LOR 252)
     1860--Republican Party--Lincoln
     Refers to demonstrators dressed in black capes
     and military helmets who paraded for Lincoln.

264. The Chloroformers. (LOR 252)

        1860--Democratic Party--Douglas
        New York supporters of Douglas who boasted they
          would put Lincoln's Wide Awakes to sleep.

265. Happiness at home and honor abroad.   (J 32)
        1860--Republican Party--Lincoln
        From the party platform.

266. Land for the Landless.   (B 408)
        1860--Republican Party--Lincoln

267. Vote Yourselves a Farm.   (B 408)
        1860--Republican Party--Lincoln
        Many of Lincoln's supporters were owners of
          small farms and landless rural voters.

268. King Cotton.   (MO, v2, 252; DAP 100)
        1860--Southern Democratic Party--Breckinridge
        Cotton was the principal crop of the South and
          seemed to southern planters to require the con-
          tinued use of slaves.

269. God, Our Country and Liberty.   (P 173)
        1860--Republican Party--Lincoln
        From an election poster.

270. Copperhead Democrats.   (LOR 261; B 451)
        1864--Democratic Party--McClellan
        The faction within the Democratic Party urging an
          immediate armistice with the South.

271. Free Speech/Free Press.   (CCB 249)
        1864--Radical Republican Party--Fremont
        Radical Republicans were opposed to a Presidential
          second term on principle.

272. Elect me President: Freedom and the Reunion of
      states shall be permanently established.   (CCB 250)
        1864--Radical Republican Party--Fremont
        From a campaign button.

273. Ironclad Oath.   (DAP 207)
        1864--Republican Party--Lincoln
        Congress had passed a law on July 2, 1862, re-
          quiring every elected official to swear he had
          never aided the enemies (i.e. the Confederates)
          of the United States.

274. No peace can be permanent without Union. (LOR 265)
    1864--Democratic Party--McClellan
    McClellan refused to accede to pressures to sue
    for an immediate armistice with the South.

275. Down with the Draft. (B 444)
    1864--Democratic Party--McClellan
    Draft rioters in 1863 encouraged the faction of the
    Democrats who urged an immediate end to the
    Civil War.

276. A rich man's war but a poor man's fight. (B 445)
    1864--Democratic Party--McClellan
    Opposition to the draft and to the continuation of
    the war had grown.

277. Our Country! (S 1189)
    1864--Republican Party--Lincoln

278. Old Abe removed McClellan--We'll now remove Old
    Abe. (B 454)
    1864--Democratic Party--McClellan
    Lincoln had removed McClellan from his command
    on November 7, 1862.

279. Mac Will Win the Union Back. (B 454)
    1864--Democratic Party--McClellan
    McClellan campaigned on a platform of reuniting
    North and South, but not on the "stop-the-war"
    platform some Democrats advocated.

280. Uncle Abe and Andy. (B 454)
    1864--Republican Party--Lincoln
    "Andy" was Andrew Johnson, Lincoln's running
    mate.

281. Vote as you shot. (B 454)
    1864--Republican Party--Lincoln

282. Don't swap horses in the middle of the stream.
    (B 454)
    1864--Republican Party--Lincoln
    An early use of this campaign slogan for a presi-
    dential second term.

283. I will be ready to swap horses, dispense law, make
    jokes, split rails. (LOR 269)

    1864--Democratic Party--McClellan
    The Democrats distributed campaign cards disparag-
    ing Lincoln by this alleged quote.

284. Freedom to All Men, Union. (CCB 208)
    1864--Republican Party--Lincoln
    Campaign button.

285. A Foe to Traitors-- / The Peoples Choice for President. (CCB 208)
    1864--Republican Party--Lincoln
    Campaign button.

286. Protection to American industry / Free homes for
  freemen. (CCB 212)
    1864--Republican Party--Lincoln
    Campaign button.

287. Lincoln and Liberty, / Good for another heat. (CCB
  217)
    1864--Republican Party--Lincoln
    Campaign button.

288. First in War, / First in Peace. (CCB 219)
    1864--Republican Party--Lincoln
    From a campaign button.

289. The voice of the people is for Little Mac. (LOR 269)
    1864--Democratic Party--McClellan
    From an election poster.

290. Proclaim Liberty / Throughout the Land. (CCB 221)
    1864--Republican Party--Lincoln
    Campaign button.

291. Abraham Lincoln, an Honest Man / The Crisis demands his re-election. (CCB 222)
    1864--Republican Party--Lincoln
    Campaign button.

292. Freedom, Justice, Truth. (CCB 224)
    1864--Republican Party--Lincoln
    From a campaign button.

293. The Great American Hesitation / Themor ucri Theles.
  (CCB 233)
    1864--Republican Party--Lincoln

An attack on McClellan whom Lincoln relieved of
his command in 1862 for hesitating to attack
Lee's army.   From a campaign button.

294.   Little Mac for President / Spades are Trumps.   (CCB
        241)
         1864--Democratic Party--McClellan
         From a campaign button.

295.   George B. McClellan--Prosperity / Union/Peace.
        (CCB 243)
         1864--Democratic Party--McClellan
         Campaign button.

296.   He lives in the hearts of his countrymen.   (Oakland,
        Calif. City Museum)
         1864--Republican Party--Lincoln
         From an election banner.

297.   My Country I am Sworn to Defend.   (CCB 236)
         1864--Democratic Party--McClellan
         McClellan dissociated himself from the Democratic
            faction which advocated immediate peace; cam-
            paigned as former commander-in-chief of the
            Union Army.   From a campaign button.

298.   The Hope of the Nation.   (CCB 236)
         1864--Democratic Party--McClellan
         Campaign button.

299.   First in the Hearts of his Soldiers.   (CCB 236)
         1864--Democratic Party--McClellan
         An appeal to the soldiers he commanded as head
            of the Union Army.   Campaign button.

300.   United States Army / Liberty & Union.   (CCB 237)
         1864--Democratic Party--McClellan
         McClellan was reminding voters that he had com-
            manded the United States Army until 1862.
            From a campaign button.

301.   The Peoples Choice for President.   (CCB 237)
         1864--Democratic Party--McClellan
         A campaign button.

302.   No compromise with armed rebels.   (CCB 209)
         1864--Republican Party--Lincoln

An attack on the Democrats who wanted immediate peace with the South. From a campaign button.

303. No compromise with traitors. (CCB 219)
    1864--Republican Party--Lincoln
    A stronger version of entry no. 302. From a campaign button.

304. May the Union flourish. (CCB 209)
    1864--Republican Party--Lincoln
    A pious hope during the dark days for the Republicans before Appomattox. From a campaign button.

305. One Flag and One Union / Now and Forever. (CCB 235)
    1864--Democratic Party--McClellan
    McClellan's supporters felt he could reunite North and South more effectively than Lincoln. From a campaign button.

306. Our Country and our Flag / Now and forever. (CCB 217)
    1864--Republican Party--Lincoln
    Many of the campaign slogans of Republicans and Democrats are interchangeable. A campaign button.

307. The Constitution and the Union / Now and forever. (CCB 213)
    1864--Republican Party--Lincoln
    A campaign button.

308. The Union must and shall be preserved. (CCB 239)
    1864--Democratic Party--McClellan
    Originally used by Andrew Jackson, also a Democrat, in 1830 (see entry no. 61). A campaign button.

309. The Union & Constitution / One & Indivisible. (CCB 234)
    1864--Democratic Party--McClellan
    Campaign button.

310. The Constitution as it is / The hope of the Union. (CCB 208)
    1864--Democratic Party--McClellan
    Campaign button.

311. The union must be preserved at all costs.   (P 176)
     1864--Democratic Party--McClellan
     Another version of entry no. 308.

312. Slavery must be abolished with reunion of states.
     (CCB 207)
     1864--Republican Party--Lincoln
     Campaign button.

313. Union and Liberty.   (CCB 228)
     1864--Republican Party--Lincoln
     Campaign button.

314. Scalawags.   (H 34)
     1868--Democratic Party--Seymour
     The Democrats' contemptuous nickname for South-
     erners who carried out Northerners' Reconstruc-
     tion policies.

315. Carpet-baggers.   (H 34)
     1868--Democratic Party--Seymour
     Democrats' nickname for Northerners carrying out
     Reconstruction policies in the South.

316. Lily Whites.   (DAP 228)
     1868--Republican Party--Grant
     Nickname for Southern Republicans who advocated
     the exclusion of black voters.

317. Forty acres and a mule.   (H 8)
     1868--Republican Party--Grant
     Freed slaves' expectations from the Republicans
     on the basis of promises from the Freedmens'
     Bureaus.

318. Grant the Butcher.   (BO 156)
     1868--Democratic Party--Seymour
     A Southern reference to Grant's Civil War ac-
     tions as general-in-chief of the United States
     Army.

319. Unconditional Surrender Grant.   (BO 155)
     1868--Republican Party--Grant

320. Repudiate the Repudiators.   (B 484)
     1868--Republican Party--Grant
     A reference to the demand by poorer farmers that

the government pay its debts in greenbacks instead of in gold.

321. Scratch a Democrat and you will Find a Rebel.
(B 484)
1868--Republican Party--Grant
Reflecting a continuing suspicion that Democrats were lukewarm about the Civil War.

322. Waving the Bloody Shirt. (DAP 40; B 484)
1868--Republican Party--Grant
Congressman Benjamin Butler once waved the bloody shirt of a "carpet-bagger" who had been flogged by the Ku Klux Klan on the floor of Congress. After that, any speaker recalling Southern violence was accused of "waving the bloody shirt."

323. The Man Who Saved the Nation. (B 484)
1868--Republican Party--Grant

324. Let us have peace. (BO 156; B 484; MO, v3, 29; CCB 257; LO 296; S 1252)
1868--Republican Party--Grant
A quote from Grant's letter accepting his nomination.

325. The party that saved the nation / Must rule it.
(B 483)
1868--Republican Party--Grant

326. Grant talks peace but makes war. (S 1260)
1868--Democratic Party--Seymour
An attempt by the Democrats to reply to Grant's "Let us have peace."

327. Radical Reconstruction. (S 1258)
1868--Republican Party--Grant
The policies of the Radical Republicans against Southerners who had acted overtly in the Confederate cause.

328. Patient of Toil / Serene amidst alarms / Inflexible in Faith / Invincible in Arms. (CCB 256)
1868--Republican Party--Grant
From a campaign button.

329. Freedom's Defender.   (CCB 259)
     1868--Republican Party--Grant
     Campaign button.

330. Liberty and Loyalty.   (CCB 260)
     1868--Republican Party--Grant
     Campaign button.

331. Soldier Statesman and Patriot.   (CCB 261)
     1868--Republican Party--Grant
     Campaign button.

332. The Will of the People is the Law of the Land.
     (CCB 261)
     1868--Republican Party--Grant
     Campaign button.

333. Gen. U. S. Grant / Our next / President / May he
     in / Wisdom rule / the Country / he has Saved.
     (CCB 265)
     1868--Republican Party--Grant
     Campaign button.

334. Grant and Colfax / Union / Liberty / and Peace.
     (CCB 275)
     1868--Republican Party--Grant
     Schuyler Colfax was Grant's running mate.   Cam-
     paign button.

335. Loyalty shall Govern / What Loyalty has Preserved.
     (CCB 281)
     1868--Republican Party--Grant
     A campaign button in support of Vice-Presidential
     candidate Colfax.

336. Loyalty shall govern the Nation.   (CCB 282)
     1868--Republican Party--Grant
     Another campaign button for Colfax.

337. No North / No South / The Union Inseparable.   (CCB
     283)
     1868--Democratic Party--Seymour
     A plea for reconciliation on a campaign button.

338. White Men to Govern, / the Restoration of Constitu-
     tional Liberty.   (CCB 284)

       1868--Democratic Party--Seymour
       An example of the intensity of racist feeling on a
       campaign button.

339. General Amnesty / Uniform currency / Equal taxes
     and / Equal Rights. (CCB 284)
       1868--Democratic Party--Seymour
       Campaign button.

340. Preservation of the Rights of the People. (CCB 285)
       1868--Democratic Party--Seymour
       Campaign button.

341. Our Choice for President. (CCB 288)
       1868--Democratic Party--Seymour
       Campaign button.

342. Constitution and Laws. (CCB 291)
       1868--Democratic Party--Seymour
       Campaign button.

343. Match him. (LOR 288)
       1868--Republican Party--Grant
       A slogan at the Republican Convention endorsing
       Grant's nomination.

344. Equal suffrage to all loyal men of the South. (LOR
     289)
       1868--Republican Party--Grant
       From the party platform, a move for reconciliation.

345. Suffrage for all, amnesty for all. (LOR 292)
       1868--Democratic Party--Seymour
       A slogan coined by Salmon P. Chase and supported
       by Seymour.

346. The Great Decliner. (LOR 296)
       1868--Republican Party--Grant
       A Republican nickname for Seymour, who first
       declined, then accepted the Democratic nomina-
       tion.

347. Reduce taxation before taxation reduces us. (LOR
     299)
       1868--Democratic Party--Seymour
       From a campaign banner.

348.   Once more to the breach and this time victory!
       (LOR 300)
              1868--Democratic Party--Seymour
              A last desperate rallying cry by August Belmont,
              Democratic Party chairman.

349.   Equality of all men before the law.   (LO 311)
              1872--Liberal Republican and Democratic Parties--
              Greeley
              From the Liberal Republican Party platform ac-
              cepted by the Democratic Party.

350.   Usurpation and corruption.   (LOR 306)
              1872--Liberal Republican and Democratic Parties--
              Greeley
              An attack on Grant for endorsing the corruption
              among his supporters.

351.   The bloody chasm.   (LOR 312)
              1872--Liberal Republican and Democratic Parties--
              Greeley
              From Greeley's acceptance of the Presidential
              nomination.

352.   Old Honesty.   (LOR 315)
              1872--Liberal Republican and Democratic Parties--
              Greeley
              Nickname for Horace Greeley.

353.   Nothing but a white hat and a white coat.   (LOR 318)
              1872--Straight Democratic & Labor Reform Parties
              --O'Conor
              Charles O'Conor's characterization of Horace
              Greeley.

354.   Some are born great / Some achieve greatness / And
       some are born in Ohio.   (B 495)
              1872--Republican Party--Grant
              A reference to Ohio's large number of electoral
              votes.

355.   Old White Hat.   (DAP 272)
              1872--Republican Party--Grant
              A jeering nickname for Greeley.

356.   Turn the Rascals Out.   (B 490)

1872--Democratic and Liberal Republican Parties--
Greeley
A reference to the corruption during Grant's first
term.

357. Grant beat Davis--Greeley bailed him.   (B 491)
1872--Republican Party--Grant
A jibe at Greeley, who was a co-signer of Jefferson Davis' bail bond.

358. Grant Us Another Term.   (B 492)
1872--Republican Party--Grant

359. Black and Tans.   (DAP 38)
1872--Republican Party--Grant
Southern Republicans who advocated voting rights
for blacks.

360. The Sage of Chappaqua.   (CCB 305)
1872--Democratic and Liberal Republican Parties--
Greeley
Campaign button.

361. The Republican Party is the ship and all else is the
sea.   (S 1321)
1872--Republican Party--Grant
A quote from black leader Frederick Douglass
expressing the suspicion of Democratic intentions
toward Southern blacks.

362. Protection to American Industry.   (CCB 295)
1872--Republican Party--Grant
Campaign button.

363. We start today upon a new march to victory.   (J 48)
1872--Republican Party--Grant
From the party platform.

364. The Champion of Popular Sovereignty.   (CCB 296)
1872--Republican Party--Grant
Campaign button.

365. The champion of amnesty, peace and plenty.   (F 54)
1872--Liberal Republican and Democratic Parties--
Greeley
From a contemporary cartoon.

366. Grant, Wilson & Prosperity. (CCB 297)
     1872--Republican Party--Grant
     Henry Wilson was Grant's running mate. Campaign
         button.

367. On to Richmond. (CCB 298)
     1872--Republican Party--Grant
     A reference to Grant's action as the Civil War
         general-in-chief. Campaign button.

368. Gold conspiracy. (H 52)
     1872--Democratic and Liberal Republican Parties--
         Greeley
     A reference to the attempt of financiers Jay Gould
         and Jim Fisk to corner the gold market with the
         connivance of Grant's intimates.

369. Vote as you fought. (H 52)
     1872--Republican Party--Grant

370. The Honest Old Farmer of Chappaqua. (CCB 302)
     1872--Liberal Republican and Democratic Parties--
         Greeley
     Campaign button.

371. Revenue Reform. Universal Amnesty. (CCB 304)
     1872--Liberal Republican and Democratic Parties--
         Greeley
     Campaign button.

372. Greeley, Brown and Reconciliation. (CCB 304)
     1872--Democratic and Liberal Republican Parties--
         Greeley
     Gratz Brown was Greeley's running mate. Cam-
         paign button.

373. The Natick Cobbler / The Galena Tanner / There's
     Nothing Like Leather. (CCB 293)
     1872--Republican Party--Grant
     Grant worked in his brother's leather store in
         Galena, Illinois after he resigned from the
         Army in 1854. Campaign button.

374. Retrenchment and Reform. (S 1390)
     1876--Democratic Party--Tilden
     A reference to blatant corruption during Grant's
         presidency.

375. Our Next President / Centennial Candidate. (CCB 315)
    1876--Republican Party--Hayes
    The year 1876 was marked by celebrations of the nation's Centennial including a Centennial Exposition in Philadelphia. Campaign button.

376. Whiskey Ring. (H 54)
    1876--Democratic Party--Tilden
    The Democratic Party attacked corruption during Grant's administrations. Whiskey distillers had blatantly defrauded the government of excise taxes.

377. Let no guilty man escape. (H 54)
    1876--Democratic Party--Tilden
    Democrats stressed that despite Grant's statement, he helped Babcock of the Whiskey Ring escape punishment.

378. Belknap Scandal. (DAP 35)
    1876--Democratic Party--Tilden
    The wife of Grant's Secretary of War was revealed to be receiving annual payoffs for selling government appointments.

379. His Fraudulency. (BO 163)
    1876--Democratic Party--Tilden
    An attack on Republican candidate Rutherford B. Hayes, whose supporters were accused of election fraud.

380. Rutherfraud B. Hayes. (BO 163)
    1876--Democratic Party--Tilden
    Another reference to election fraud allegations.

381. The Usurper. (BO 163)
    1876--Democratic Party--Tilden
    The Republicans were accused of a fraudulent deal with Southern Democrats.

382. Hurrah! For Hayes and Honest Ways! (B 496)
    1876--Republican Party--Hayes
    Not many voters believed the election was honest.

383. The Boys in Blue Will See It Through. (B 496)
    1876--Republican Party--Hayes
    An appeal to Northern veterans of the Civil War.

384. Avoid Rebel Rule. (B 496)
     1876--Republican Party--Hayes
     A reference to lukewarm support of the Civil War
     by some Democrats.

385. Plumed Knight. (MO, v3, 36; LO 328; B 495)
     1876--Republican Party--Hayes
     Congressman James G. Blaine was described as a
     "Plumed Knight" by Robert Ingersoll, who nomi-
     nated him for the Presidency. Although Blaine
     was the favorite, Hayes won the nomination.

386. Invisible in war, invincible in peace. (B 494)
     1876--Republican Party--Hayes
     Blaine's opponents' description of the "Plumed
     Knight."

387. The Aggressive Leader of Reform--Samuel J. Tilden.
     (CCB 321)
     1876--Democratic Party--Tilden
     Campaign button.

388. That eternal vigilance which is the price of liberty.
     (J 49)
     1876--Democratic Party--Tilden
     From the party platform.

389. A change of system, a change of administration, a
     change of parties, a change of measures and of men.
     (J 51)
     1876--Democratic Party--Tilden
     From the party platform.

390. I don't care about your piece of cake, but I must
     show you my sore toe. (CCB 320)
     1876--Republican Party--Hayes
     A sneering reference to Tilden's preoccupation
     with his poor health. He carried a medicine
     chest with him throughout the campaign. Cam-
     paign button.

391. National reform. (S 1391)
     1876--Democratic Party--Tilden
     The Democrats persistently attacked Republican
     corruption during Grant's administration.

392. Good government, good-will and good money. (S 1400)
     1876--Democratic Party--Tilden

393. The War Claims of the South. (S 1403)
     1876--Republican Party--Hayes
     The Republicans were charging that Tilden would
     give in to the South and overturn the Civil War
     victory of the North.

394. New policy. (S 1425)
     1876--Republican Party--Hayes
     The Republicans promised a new strong but equit-
     able and conciliatory policy in the South.

395. "New Departure" politics. (S 1427)
     1876--Republican Party--Hayes
     A promise of new fiscal policies and a new policy
     in the South.

396. Free silver. (H 149)
     1876--Greenback Party--Cooper

397. He serves his party best who serves the country best.
     (H 145; S 1425)
     1876--Republican Party--Hayes

398. Of the two evils choose the least. (D 165)
     1876--Republican Party--Hayes
           Democratic Party--Tilden
     From a widely distributed campaign card.

399. No Monopoly--Workingmen's Rights. (Z 245)
     1876--Workingmen's Party (later the Socialist
     Labor Party)

400. The Democratic Party is a party of famine. (LOR
     359)
     1880--Republican Party--Garfield
     An attack on the Democrats from a speech by
     Republican orator Robert Ingersoll.

401. The Stalwarts. (LOR 339)
     1880--Republican Party--Garfield
     Conservative wing of the party, led by Senator
     Roscoe Conkling, supporting the nomination of
     Grant.

402. The Half-Breeds. (LOR 339)
     1880--Republican Party--Garfield
     Liberal wing of the party supporting James G.
     Blaine for nomination.

403. Solid South. (LOR 341)
     1880--Democratic Party--Hancock
     The South's solid vote for the Democratic Party
     became a continuing tradition.

404. Yellow Peril. (B 501)
     1880--Republican Party--Garfield
     Prejudice and recurrent violence against Chinese
     and Japanese immigrants found expression in
     this widely used slogan.

405. Old Guard. (DAP 272)
     1880--Republican Party--Garfield
     Another nickname for the Republican faction that
     favored the nomination of Grant (see entry no.
     401).

406. Three twenty nine. (BO 169; LOR 361)
     1880--Democratic Party--Hancock
     An attack on Garfield, who had received $329 as
     a dividend from Credit Mobilier, which was re-
     vealed as a fraudulent company.

407. James A Garfield / the / Nation's choice for Presi-
     dent. (CCB 327)
     1880--Republican Party--Garfield
     Campaign button.

408. A Superb Soldier / A Model President. (CCB 334)
     1880--Democratic Party--Hancock
     Campaign button.

409. And when asked what State he hails from / Our sole
     reply shall be / He hails from Appomattox / And its
     famous apple tree. (S 1527)
     1880--Republican Party--Garfield
     The opening of Roscoe Conkling's nominating speech
     for Grant later changed slightly and adapted as
     a slogan for Garfield.

410. Hancock the superb! (LO 354; S 1503)
     1880--Democratic Party--Hancock
     A description of Hancock by his commanding offi-
     cer, McClellan, during the Civil War.

411. Honest money, consisting of gold and silver. (S 1504)
     1880--Democratic Party--Hancock
     An attack on greenback demands.

412. A tariff for revenue only. (S 1504)
     1880--Democratic Party--Hancock
     Democrats opposed protectionist tariffs.

413. Purity & patriotism. (S 1504)
     1880--Republican Party--Garfield
     A feeble attempt to counter accusations of corruption and to attack Democrats for Civil War rebellion.

414. A free ballot, a fair count and equality of all classes. (S 1506)
     1880--Greenback Labor Party--Weaver

415. A pound of pluck is worth a ton of luck. (S 1507)
     1880--Republican Party--Garfield

416. In the Union War I fought so well / That my name is greeted with the "rebel yell." (S 1508)
     1880--Republican Party--Garfield
     An attack on Democratic candidate Hancock for his Civil War record.

417. The friend of labor and the laboring man. (J 57)
     1880--Democratic Party--Hancock
     From the party platform.

418. A public office is a public trust. (DAP 311; LO 393; BO 178; CCB 348)
     1884--Democratic Party--Cleveland
     This quote from Cleveland was repeated over and over again by his supporters and used on campaign posters and buttons.

419. Rum, Romanism and Rebellion. (LO 386)
     1884--Democratic Party--Cleveland
     When Blaine did not repudiate this statement by one of his supporters, Democrats denounced Blaine as anti-Catholic.

420. Ma, Ma, Where's my Pa? / Gone to the White House / Ha! Ha! Ha! (PO 123; LO 385)
     1884--Republican Party--Blaine
     A Republican jingle attacking Cleveland for fathering an illegitimate child.

421. Blaine! Blaine! James G. Blaine! / The con-tin-en-tal

liar from the state of Maine.   (H 204; LO 383)
1884--Democratic Party--Cleveland
An anti-Blaine jingle.

422.   Reform--Cleveland.   (CCB 342)
1884--Democratic Party--Cleveland
A campaign button.

423.   Cleveland and Hendricks on a Broad Platform of Good
Planks / Will lead all to Victory.   (CCB 344)
1884--Democratic Party--Cleveland
A campaign button.   Thomas Hendricks was Cleveland's running mate.

424.   Protection to American Industry.   (CCB 350)
1884--Republican Party--Blaine
Campaign button (see entry no. 362).

425.   The Republicans have ruled since 1860 and with Blaine
and Logan, are good for another term.   (CCB 356)
1884--Republican Party--Blaine
A campaign button.   John Logan was Blaine's running mate.

426.   Protection, no British pauper wages for Americans.
(CCB 355)
1884--Republican Party--Blaine
A bit of Anglophobia as well as a campaign slogan
(on a button) for protectionism.

427.   We will follow where the white plume waves.   (CCB
355)
1884--Republican Party--Blaine
Blaine had been dubbed "The Plumed Knight" by
Ingersoll in 1876 (see entry no. 385).   Campaign button.

428.   Belshazzar Blaine.   (S 1604)
1884--Democratic Party--Cleveland
An attack on Blaine, who was accused of giving an
opulent banquet ignoring the plight of the poor.

429.   Burn this letter!   Burn this letter! / Kind regards to
Mrs. Fisher.   (LOR 382; S 1574)
1884--Democratic Party--Cleveland
Democrats made widespread use of a quote from a
letter of Blaine's to Warren Fisher which included damaging facts.

430. We love him for the enemies he has made. (DU 183)
     1884--Democratic Party--Cleveland
     Said by Edward Bragg, a Wisconsin delegate to the
     Democratic Convention, and adopted by the
     Democrats as a campaign slogan against Tam-
     many.

431. Tell the truth. (LOR 384)
     1884--Democratic Party--Cleveland
     Cleveland's response when supporters asked him
     how to handle the story of his illegitimate child.

432. Mugwump. (DAP 250)
     1884--Democratic Party--Cleveland
     The nickname for Republicans who opposed Blaine
     and defected to the Democratic candidate.

433. All unnecessary taxation is unjust taxation. (J 78)
     1884--Democratic Party--Cleveland

434. Tippecanoe and Morton too. (CCB 387)
     1888--Republican Party--Harrison
     The Republican candidate was Benjamin Harrison,
     grandson of William Henry, "Old Tippecanoe."
     His running mate was Levi Morton. Campaign
     button.

435. Veto President. (BO 180; MO, v3, 46)
     1888--Republican Party--Harrison
     A Republican nickname for Cleveland, who had
     vetoed a $10,000 appropriation to distribute
     seed in Texas during a drought.

436. Protection of American Labor. (CCB 387)
     1888--Republican Party--Harrison
     The Republicans advocated high protectionist
     tariffs. Campaign button.

437. Free Trade. (CCB 391)
     1888--Democratic Party--Cleveland
     Democrats opposed protectionist tariffs. Cam-
     paign button.

438. When Grover Goes Marching Home. (F 72)
     1888--Republican Party--Harrison
     A Republican campaign song predicting Cleveland's
     defeat.

439. Protection: We will support the interests of America. (F 74)
    1888--Republican Party--Harrison
    Slogan on a paper lantern used in campaign parades.

440. For God, for Home and Native Land. (CCB 404)
    1888--Prohibition Party--Fisk
    Campaign button.

441. Prohibition / Victory. (CCB 405)
    1888--Prohibition Party--Fisk
    Campaign button.

442. The Product of Labor / Belongs to the Producers. (CCB 405)
    1888--Union Labor Party--Streeter
    A campaign button.

443. Blaine, Blaine, James G. Blaine / We've had him once and we'll have him again. (LOR 396)
    1888--Republican Party--Harrison
    A slogan in favor of Blaine before and during the Convention until Harrison was nominated.

444. Grandfather's Hat Fits Ben. (BO 183; DAP 177)
    1888--Republican Party--Harrison
    Benjamin Harrison was William Henry Harrison's grandson.

445. Don't, don't, don't be afraid / Only low tariff so don't be afraid. (LO 405)
    1888--Democratic Party--Cleveland
    Democrats advocated free trade.

446. Trade, trade no free trade. (LO 405)
    1888--Republican Party--Harrison
    Republicans advocated protectionist tariffs.

447. The English Candidate. (LOR 404)
    1888--Republican Party--Harrison
    Republican nickname for Cleveland when the British minister, Sir Lionel Sackville-West, wrote that Democrats were more friendly to England than Republicans.

448. Your Wages under Free Trade / What matter if Prices are Reduced / Wages Drop to Free Trade

Levels? (CCB 368)
1888--Republican Party--Harrison
A campaign button.

449. Fraternity--Charity--Loyalty. (CCB 369)
1888--Republican Party--Harrison
Campaign button.

450. Protection to Home Industries. (CCB 372)
1888--Republican Party--Harrison
The insistent Republican issue of high protectionist
tariffs. Campaign button.

451. Beast of Buffalo. (S 1622)
1888--Republican Party--Harrison
A Republican characterization of Democratic candidate, Cleveland, who had been mayor of Buffalo.

452. Good government. (S 1615)
1888--Democratic Party--Cleveland

453. Billion Dollar Congress. (LOR 407; DAP 37)
1892--Republican Party--Harrison
The 51st Congress was the first to make more
than a billion dollars in appropriations, but the
Speaker boasted this was a "billion dollar country."

454. Three acres and a cow. (DAP 374)
1892--People's Party (Populists)--Weaver
The People's Party campaigned for small farmers
and against the abuses of the railroads.

455. Goodbye, Party Bosses. (B 591)
1892--People's Party (Populists)--Weaver

456. Free Wool to Make Our Breeches. (B 591)
1892--Democratic Party--Cleveland
Democrats campaigned for free trade.

457. Drive the High-Tariff Tinkers to the Wall. (B 591)
1892--Democratic Party--Cleveland
Another attack on the high tariff protectionism of
the Republicans.

458. Goodbye, Free Traders, Goodbye. (B 591)

1892--Repuglican Party--Harrison
The Republicans advocated high protectionist tariffs.

459. Hail Protection. (B 591)
1892--Republican Party--Harrison
See entry nos. 456, 457, 458.

460. Grover, Grover, / Four more years of Grover / Out they go, in we go / Then we'll be in clover. (B 590; S 1717)
1892--Democratic Party--Cleveland

461. If any will not work, neither shall he eat. (LO 419)
1892--People's Party (Populists)--Weaver
The People's Party included elements from Farmers Alliances, Greenbackers, Socialists and trade unionists.

462. Wealth belongs to him who creates it, and every dollar taken from industry without an equivalent is robbery. (LO 419)
1892--People's Party (Populists)--Weaver

463. Grover, Grover, All is over. (B 590)
1892--Republican Party--Harrison

464. Antisnapper. (S 1730)
1892--Democratic Party--Cleveland
Democrats who opposed Tammany and the so-called "snap" convention which nominated David Hill instead of Cleveland.

465. Adlai and his Axe! (S 1730)
1892--Republican Party--Harrison
An attack on Cleveland's running mate, Adlai Stevenson, whose personnel cuts in the Post Office rankled.

466. The Prophet and the ballot box--both stuffed. (S 1723)
1892--Republican Party--Harrison
A gibe at Cleveland, who weighed 250 pounds.

467. Let every honest fellow from Maine to Oregon / Let every honest fellow, unless he's a son-of-a-gun, / Be sure and vote for Benjamin Harrison. (S 1715)
1892--Republican--Harrison

468. No Force Bill! No Negro Domination! (S 1730)
      1892--Democratic Party--Cleveland
      A slogan of the Southern Democrats supporting
      Cleveland.

469. Raise less corn and more hell. (MO, v3, 105; LOR
      408; S 1907)
      1892--People's Party (Populists)--Weaver
      From a speech by Mary Elizabeth Lease, no mean
      hellraiser herself.

470. None but Democrats on guard. (S 1712)
      1892--Democratic Party--Cleveland
      A slogan from Governor David Hill of New York,
      who aspired to the Democratic nomination but
      lost to Cleveland.

471. The Twelve Apostles. (S 1708)
      1892--Republican Party--Harrison
      A joking reference to the prominent Republicans
      who pushed for Harrison's renomination.

472. The People's Choice. (S 1708)
      1892--Republican Party--Harrison
      Some of the convention delegates still supported
      Blaine and wore badges with this slogan, but
      Blaine refused to run.

473. Advance agent of prosperity. (H 274; LOR 432)
      1896--Republican Party--McKinley
      Billboards across the country paid for by Mark
      Hanna hailed McKinley as the agent of prosper-
      ity during a depression.

474. Sound Money. (LOR 433)
      1896--Republican Party--McKinley
      The Republican Party platform advocated the gold
      standard.

475. The dollar of our daddies, / of silver coinage free,
      / Will make us rich and happy / Will bring prosper-
      ity. (H 267)
      1896--Democratic and Populist Parties--Bryan

476. Patriotism, Protection, and Prosperity. (Election
      Poster, Oakland, Calif. Museum)
      1896--Republican Party--McKinley

477. The full dinner pail. (B 600; LO 445; DAP 168; S
     1819; DU 199; M 15)
       1896--Republican Party--McKinley
       The Republicans campaigned on promises to return
         the country to prosperity.

478. Stop Bryan, Save America. (B 601)
       1896--Republican Party--McKinley
       Bryan, the Democratic and Populist candidate, was
         being pictured as a dangerous zealot.

479. In God We Trust, With Bryan We Bust. (B 600)
       1896--Republican Party--McKinley

480. You shall not press down upon the brow of labor this
     crown of thorns, you shall not crucify mankind upon a
     cross of gold. (B 600; LO 440)
       1896--Democratic Party & Populist Party--Bryan

481. We'll All Have Our Pockets Lined With Silver.
     (B 600)
       1896--Democratic Party & Populist Party--Bryan
       Bryan campaigned on the free silver issue.

482. Front porch campaign. (LOR 431; DAP 168)
       1896--Republican Party--McKinley
       In contrast to Bryan's whirlwind campaigning,
         McKinley remained at home receiving delega-
         tions on his front porch in Canton, Ohio.

483. The Great Commoner. (A 458; B 222)
       1896--Democratic Party & Populist Party--Bryan
       The universal nickname for Bryan.

484. Stand Pat with McKinley. (B 76)
       1896--Republican Party--McKinley

485. The Boy Orator of the Platte. (A 475; DU 199; B 222;
     DAP 44)
       1896--Democratic Party & Populist Party--Bryan
       Bryan from Nebraska was only 36 and already
         known as a fiery speaker.

486. We defy them. (LO 440)
       1896--Democratic Party & Populist Party--Bryan
       From Bryan's speech at the Democratic Party Con-
         vention. He was defying those he called "idle

holders of idle capital." See entry no. 480 for
another slogan from the same speech.

487. Sixteen to one. (DAP 346)
    1896--Democratic Party & Populist Party--Bryan
    Bryan ran on a campaign of free coinage of silver
    at a ratio of 16 ounces of silver to one of gold.

488. Free Silver. (LO 456)
    1896--Democratic Party & Populist Party--Bryan

489. Principles First. (S 1807)
    1896--Democratic Party & Populist Party--Bryan

490. Gold, gold, gold / I love to hear it jingle / Gold, gold,
    gold / Its power is untold / The women they adore it /
    While the men try hard to store it / There is not a bet-
    ter thing in life than / Gold, gold gold. (S 1802)
    1896--Republican Party--McKinley

491. The People Against the Bosses. (S 1800)
    1896--Democratic Party & Populist Party--Bryan

492. Dollar Mark. (LOR 440)
    1896--Democratic Party & Populist Party--Bryan
    An attack against millionaire Mark Hanna, who
    managed McKinley's campaign.

493. Good money never made hard times. (BAR 30)
    1896--Republican Party--McKinley

494. The Honest Little Dollar's Here to Stay. (BAR 30)
    1896--Republican Party--McKinley
    From a McKinley campaign song.

495. The Peerless Leader. (LOR 452)
    1896--Democratic Party--Bryan
    A Democratic characterization of Bryan.

496. The hero of San Juan Hill. (LOR 455)
    1900--Republican Party--McKinley
    The nickname of Theodore Roosevelt, McKinley's
    running mate.

497. To hell with Spain. (B 617)
    1900--Republican Party--McKinley
    A slogan during the War with Spain which was re-
    called during the 1900 campaign.

498. Don't dishonor the flag by hauling it down.   (B 625)
     1900--Republican Party--McKinley
     Another slogan from the War in Cuba in which
        McKinley's running mate, Theodore Roosevelt,
        had fought.

499. Splendid little war.   (B 627)
     1900--Republican Party--McKinley
     From a letter by John Hay to his friend Theodore
        Roosevelt, McKinley's running mate, about the
        War with Spain in 1898.

500. Remember the Maine.   (MO, v3, 118; DU 203; DAP
     324; B 617)
     1900--Republican Party--McKinley
     The Maine was sunk on February 15, 1898, and
        precipitated the War with Spain.   Republicans
        took credit for a quick and victorious end to
        the war.

501. Benevolent Assimilation.   (DAP 35)
     1900--Republican Party--McKinley
     The Republicans put forward this motivation for
        the United States' annexation of the Philippines.

502. Open Door Policy.   (DAP 273; B 632; MO, v3, 125)
     1900--Republican Party--McKinley
     McKinley's Secretary of State, John Hay, enunciated
        this as the policy of the United States in 1899,
        a denial of imperialist intentions in China.

503. The Millionaires' Club.   (B 664)
     1900--Republican Party--McKinley
     A characterization of the United States Senate.

504. Let Well Enough Alone.   (H 338; S 1885; B 635)
     1900--Republican Party--McKinley

505. Continue prosperity by voting for McKinley and Roose-
     velt.   (LOR 459)
     1900--Republican Party--McKinley
     From a campaign banner.

506. Lincoln abolished slavery, McKinley has restored it.
     (LO 460)
     1900--Democratic Party--Bryan
     Bryan claimed that the Republicans' protective

tariffs and gold standard were improverishing and enslaving the working men.

507. The Flag of the Republic forever; / of an Empire Never! (LO 460)
1900--Democratic Party--Bryan
Bryan opposed the growing imperialism of the Republicans.

508. Prosperity at home, prestige abroad, sound money. (LO 466)
1900--Republican Party--McKinley

509. It's better to be President than to be right! (LO 450)
1900--Democratic Party--Bryan
The Democrats claimed that Mark Hanna manipulated McKinley and that Hanna was reversing Clay's statement. (See entry no. 189)

510. Independence and self-government for Cuba. (LOR 461)
1900--Republican Party--McKinley
From the party platform.

511. Four More Years of the Full Dinner Pail. (LOR 456; M 17)
1900--Republican Party--McKinley
(See entry no. 477.)

512. The Strenuous Life. (S 1908)
1900--Republican Party--McKinley
In a speech in 1899 Roosevelt used this phrase. The speech was widely distributed during the 1900 campaign.

513. To impose upon any people a government of force is to substitute the methods of imperialism for those of a republic. (J 112)
1900--Democratic Party--Bryan
From the party platform.

514. No nation can long endure half republic and half empire. Imperialism abroad will lead quickly and inevitably to despotism at home. (J 112)
1900--Democratic Party--Bryan
From the party platform.

515. Unceasing warfare against private monopoly. (J 114)
    1900--Democratic Party--Bryan
    From the party platform.

516. Establish the Co-operative Commonwealth. (J 127)
    1900--Social Democratic Party--Eugene V. Debs
    From the party platform.

517. The Rough Rider. (LOR 458)
    1900--Republican Party--McKinley
    A reference to the Army service of Vice-
        Presidential candidate Roosevelt during the War
        in Cuba, 1898.

518. Theodore! With all thy faults. (LOR 480)
    1904--Republican Party--Roosevelt
    A five-word editorial in the conservative New York
        Sun which became a campaign slogan.

519. I took the Canal Zone and let Congress debate.
    (DU 206; LOR 478)
    1904--Republican Party--Roosevelt
    Roosevelt boasted that he had helped engineer a
        coup and quickly signed a treaty with the new
        government which opened the way for the Pan-
        ama Canal.

520. The safe and sane candidate. (LO 485)
    1904--Democratic Party--Parker
    The Democrats repudiated the policies advocated
        by Bryan, who was considered too radical by
        influential Democratic supporters.

521. Square Deal. (A 466)
    1904--Republican Party--Roosevelt
    When Lincoln Steffens remonstrated with him for
        not dealing with fundamental issues, Roosevelt
        said he was for a "square deal" and that would
        be his slogan.

522. Square Deal for Labor. (B 650)
    1904--Republican Party--Roosevelt
    Roosevelt extended his slogan in sympathy with
        some of labor's demands but he remained un-
        friendly to labor unions.

523. Trust-buster. (Z 342)

1904--Republican Party--Roosevelt
Roosevelt prided himself on his record as President in controlling the arrogant trusts.

524. Speak softly and carry a big stick. (LO 480; DAP 36)
1904--Republican Party--Roosevelt
Roosevelt used this African proverb to describe his
approach to United States foreign policy.

525. Boom, boom, boom, / First, first, first; / California, California / Hearst, Hearst, Hearst. (S 1978)
1904--Democratic Party--Parker
William Randolph Hearst's supporters urged his
nomination at the Convention before Alton Parker
was chosen.

526. Perdicaris alive or Raisuli dead. (LO 485; S 1971)
1904--Republican Party--Roosevelt
A reference to one of Roosevelt's "Big Stick" ac-
tions. When an American (Perdicaris) was kid-
napped by a Moroccan (Raisuli), Roosevelt
threatened punitive action.

527. The Do-Something Party. (S 1971)
1904--Republican Party--Roosevelt
From a speech by Speaker of the House Joseph
Cannon in support of Roosevelt's candidacy.

528. Three Cheers for the Rough Rider. (B 657)
1904--Republican Party--Roosevelt
A reference to Roosevelt's participation in the
Spanish-American War in 1898.

529. The unconditional surrender of the capitalist class.
(J 143; S 2069)
1904--Socialist Labor Party--Corregan
From the party platform. Used again in 1908 and
in 1916.

530. A government of law, not of men. (B 657)
1904--Democratic Party--Parker

531. Don't flinch, don't foul, hit the line hard. (LO 491)
1904--Republican Party--Roosevelt
Roosevelt was fond of sports metaphors, part of
his "Strenuous Life" advocacy.

532. Workers Unite. (LO 481)
    1904--Socialist Party--Debs
    Debs campaigned actively throughout the country.
    From a campaign banner.

533. More prosperity. (LO 481)
    1904--Republican Party--Roosevelt
    The Republicans boasted of the prosperity they had
    created in the previous administration and prom-
    ised still more of the same.

534. A return to Jeffersonian principles. (LO 481)
    1904--Democratic Party--Parker
    Having turned from Bryan's impassioned and color-
    ful oratory, the Democrats ran a lackluster cam-
    paign.

535. Malefactors of great wealth. (LO 481)
    1904--Republican Party--Roosevelt
    Roosevelt coined this slogan as part of his "trust
    buster" image.

536. Votes for Women. (B 665)
    1908--Democratic Party--Bryan
    Suffragists appeared at the Democratic Convention
    presenting demands for women's suffrage. This
    is the first time women were officially seated as
    delegates, but their demands went unheeded.

537. Taxation Without Representation. (B 665)
    1908--Democratic Party--Bryan
    (See entry no. 536.)

538. Equal Suffrage for Men and Women. (B 665)
    1908--Democratic Party--Bryan
    (See entry no. 536.)

539. The Democratic Party Must Be Progressive. (S 2055)
    1908--Democratic Party--Bryan
    Bryan was trying to revitalize the Party after "safe
    and sane" Parker's defeat.

540. Big Bill. (DU 218)
    1908--Republican Party--William Howard Taft
    A nickname referring to Taft's size. He weighed
    330 pounds.

541. My little brown brothers. (DU 218)
    1908--Republican Party--Taft
    Taft as Governor of the Philippines had used this
      phrase, which was picked up as an example of
      his good nature.

542. Smile, Smile, Smile. (BAR 223)
    1908--Republican Party--Taft
    Taft's campaign motto. He was known as the most
      jovial man in politics.

543. Yellow Peril. (L 153)
    1908--Democratic Party--Bryan
    The old xenophobic slogan (see entry no. 404) was
      being used frequently once more by the Hearst
      press.

544. The man worthwhile with the big glad smile. (BAR
223)
    1908--Republican Party--Taft
    From a campaign song.

545. Shall the people rule? (S 2077; J 144; LO 499)
    1908--Democratic Party--Bryan
    From the party platform (see entry no. 40).

546. Democracy would have the nation own the people, while
Republicanism would have the people own the nation.
(J 163)
    1908--Republican Party--Taft
    From the party platform.

547. Grand in Peace, Brave in War, / Lovingly in the
Hearts of His Countrymen. (F 97)
    1908--Democratic Party--Bryan
    A campaign poster comparing Bryan with George
      Washington.

548. Rum, Romanism and Capitalism. (S 2087)
    1908--Republican Party--Taft
    Bryan's supporters claimed he had been defeated
      by a combination of anti-Catholics, Prohibition-
      ists, and big business.

549. Romanism, Roosevelt and Rockefeller. (S 2089)
    1908--Republican Party--Taft
    Bryan's supporters blamed his defeat on anti-

Catholics (Romanism), Teddy Roosevelt (who supported Taft), and Rockefeller (representative of big business).

550. Wall Street gold and Jesuitical conspiracy. (S 2089)
1908--Republican Party--Taft
Bryan's supporters claimed Wall Street Capitalists and rabid anti-Catholics defeated him.

551. Catholicism, Commercialism and Coercion. (S 2089)
1908--Republican Party--Taft
Bryan's supporters claimed he had been defeated by a combination of anti-Catholics, Big Business, and corrupt use of money by the Republicans.

552. Four-four-four years more. (S 2072)
1908--Republican Party--Taft
At the Republican Convention supporters of Roosevelt pushed for his nomination but he had promised not to run again and reluctantly supported Taft.

553. My hat is in the ring. (LOR 510)
1912--Progressive Party--Roosevelt
Despite his 1904 announcement that he would not run again, Roosevelt announced his determination to run with this slogan.

554. The great privileged interests. (LOR 511)
1912--Progressive Party--Roosevelt
Roosevelt accused Taft of having given in to the rich.

555. Muckrakers. (B 660; DAP 250)
1912--Progressive Party--Roosevelt
Roosevelt had coined this term for reformers in 1906. By 1912 he was touting himself as a reformer.

556. New Freedom. (H 442; B 702; DAP 263; LOR 521)
1912--Democratic Party--Wilson
Wilson's version of Roosevelt's "New Nationalism." The slogan was from the title of Wilson's book.

557. The Moose Is Loose. (B 683)
1912--Progressive Party--Roosevelt
The symbol for the new party was the bull moose (see entry no. 563).

558. We're Ready for Teddy Again. (B 683)
    1912--Progressive Party--Roosevelt
    When Roosevelt failed to capture the Republican
        nomination, he ran as the candidate of the new
        third party.

559. Wilson--That's All. (B 683)
    1912--Democratic Party--Wilson
    A succinct slogan.

560. Row, Row, Woodrow. (B 683)
    1912--Democratic Party--Wilson

561. Toot, toot, Toot, toot! (LOR 518)
    1912--Republican Party--Taft
    At the Republican Convention, supporters of Roose-
        velt used this shouted slogan to show opposition
        to convention chairman Elihu Root, who supported
        Taft. The cry was a play on Root's name and a
        supposed imitation of a steamroller.

562. New Nationalism. (LO 523; BO 199; H 430)
    1912--Progressive Party--Roosevelt
    Roosevelt's phrase for the new vigorous policies he
        proposed to follow.

563. Strong as a bull moose. (LO 523)
    1912--Progressive Party--Roosevelt
    Roosevelt announced his return to active politics
        with this phrase, which became the byword for
        his campaign.

564. Fight in honorable fashion for the good of mankind.
    (LO 510)
    1912--Progressive Party--Roosevelt

565. What this country needs is a really good five-cent
    cigar. (LO 510)
    1912--Democratic Party--Wilson
    A remark by Vice-Presidential candidate Thomas
        Marshall which has been used cynically ever
        since.

566. A religious cult with a fakir at the head of it. (BAR
    126)
    1912--Republican Party--Taft
    Taft's exasperated evaluation of Roosevelt and the
        Progressive Party.

567. Extirpation of corruption, fraud, and machine rule in American politics. (J 175)
1912--Democratic Party--Wilson
From the party platform.

568. A government of laws, not of men. (J 183)
1912--Republican Party--Taft
From the party platform.

569. Set the public welfare in the first place. (J 175)
1912--Progressive Party--Roosevelt
From the party platform.

570. Dollar Diplomacy. (L 154; DAP 125)
1912--Republican Party--Taft
United States diplomacy during Taft's administration which supported United States business expansion in China and in Central America. Loans, intervention, support to rebels and outright protectorates were all used to further U.S. business interests.

571. Even a rat in a corner will fight. (M 102)
1912--Progressive Party--Roosevelt
From a speech by Taft and used by Roosevelt against Taft.

572. Age of Reform. (Z 341)
1912--Progressive Party--Roosevelt
Roosevelt's characterization of the period and of the role he perceived for the new party.

573. Progressive Period. (Z 341)
1912--Progressive Party--Roosevelt
Roosevelt felt the new party epitomized the new age.

574. Give the government back to the people. (L 88)
1912--Progressive Party--Roosevelt

575. We stand at Armageddon, and we battle for the Lord. (DAP 24; H 437; M 126; LO 510)
1912--Progressive Party--Roosevelt
From a fiery speech by Roosevelt the night before the balloting at the Republican Convention which chose Taft.

576. A dead cock in a pit. (BAR 126)

       1912--Progressive Party--Roosevelt
       Roosevelt's description of his former friend Taft.

577. The Charter of Democracy. (DAP 59)
       1912--Progressive Party--Roosevelt
       On February 11, 1912 Roosevelt put forward the
         personal platform he later advocated as Pro-
         gressive Party candidate.

578. A Covenant with the People. (DAP 104)
       1912--Progressive Party--Roosevelt
       From the introduction to the party platform.

579. Dominant Americanism. (LOR 529)
       1916--Republican Party--Hughes

580. Watchful Waiting. (B 703; DAP 401; LOR 526)
       1916--Democratic Party--Wilson
       Wilson's policy toward the Huerta government of
         Mexico before sending United States Marines to
         Vera Cruz in 1914.

581. A land redeemed from drink. (J 204)
       1916--Prohibition Party--Hanly
       From the party platform.

582. Too proud to fight. (Z 352; DU 228; DAP 375)
       1916--Democratic Party--Wilson
       Wilson's response when the Lusitania was sunk on
         May 10, 1915, and his stance during the 1916
         election.

583. A strict and honest neutrality. (J 204)
       1916--Republican Party--Hughes
       From the party platform.

584. Wilson and Peace with honor / Or Hughes with Roose-
     velt and war. (LO 544; B 720; BAR 130)
       1916--Democratic Party--Wilson
       Democrats accused Republicans of being the War
         Party.

585. You are Working--Not Fighting / Alive and Happy--
     Not Cannon Fodder. (LO 544; B 720)
       1916--Democratic Party--Wilson
       A reference to Wilson's refusal to enter the war.

586. He kept us out of war. (BAR 228; J 200; LO 539)
     1916--Democratic Party--Wilson
     The Democrats' campaign slogan taken from the
     Party platform.

587. I didn't raise my boy to be a soldier. (B 717; Z 363)
     1916--Democratic Party--Wilson
     From a popular song.

588. International brotherhood, world peace and industrial
     democracy. (S 2287)
     1916--Socialist Party--Benson
     From the party platform.

589. Peace with Honor and Continued Prosperity. (S 2267)
     1916--Democratic Party--Wilson
     Wilson campaigned as the peace candidate.

590. Teddy, Teddy, Everybody's for Teddy. (B 719)
     1916--Republican Party--Hughes
     A slogan of those at the Republican Convention who
     supported Roosevelt's nomination.

591. America Needs Hughes. (BAR 132)
     1916--Republican Party--Hughes
     Roosevelt's support for Hughes.

592. America first and America efficient. (BAR 129)
     1916--Republican Party--Hughes.

593. Preparedness--not for war but only for defense.
     (Campaign banner in archive film)
     1916--Democratic Party--Wilson
     Wilson proposed that the United States adopt a pol-
     icy of armed neutrality.

594. Who broke the money trust? / Who kept us out of
     war? (From an archive film)
     1916--Democratic Party--Wilson

595. GOP--not dead but dying. (From an archive film)
     1916--Democratic Party--Wilson

596. A peace without victory. (L 189)
     1917--Democratic Party--Wilson
     In January 1917 Wilson still hoped for a negotiated

peace without indemnities or annexation of territory.

597. A little group of willful men. (L 190)
1917--Democratic Party--Wilson
In February 1917 Wilson railed against the Senators who filibustered against his bill authorizing the arming of merchant vessels.

598. A war to end all wars. (Z 355)
1917--Wilson
On April 6, 1917, Congress declared war.

599. Force, force to the utmost. (B 727)
1917--Wilson
After the declaration of war Wilson urged rapid arming for a quick end to the war.

600. A war to make the world safe for democracy.
(B 727; Z 355)
1917--Wilson
A promise that was unfulfilled.

601. Fourteen Points. (B 728)
1918--Wilson
Wilson urged settlement of World War I around a document containing 14 sections to which all the belligerents would agree.

602. Open covenants openly arrived at. (DAP 272)
1918--Wilson
One of the Fourteen Points Wilson was urging.

603. National self-determination. (DAP 258)
1918--Wilson
Wilson advocated a new approach to nationalism.

604a. Hang the Kaiser
  b. Keep the Home Fires Burning
  c. A Woman's Place Is in the War
  d. Work--or Fight
  e. Fuel Will Win the War
  f. Rivets Are Bayonets--Drive Them Home
  g. Give Until It Hurts
  h. Lafayette--We Are Here
  i. The Yanks Are Coming
        1917-1918. Slogans popular in the United States

during World War I. From songs, banners, posters, films of the period.

605. Freed from Demon Rum. (DU 235)
1920--Prohibition Party--Watkins
In 1920 the Prohibition Party realized its long sought goal--passage of the 18th Amendment.

606. I cannot say no. (DU 237)
1920--Republican Party--Harding
Harding was so congenial that he said of himself, if he were a woman he'd always be pregnant.

607. For Americanism and Nationalism / Against Internationalism. (LOR 543)
1920--Republican Party--Harding
From Senator Henry Cabot Lodge's speech at the Convention.

608. The Noble experiment. (L 305; DU 235)
1920--Prohibition Party--Watkins
After a wartime prohibition act, the 18th Amendment to the Constitution was passed in 1920.

609. Peace, disarmament and world fraternity. (S 2362)
1920--Democratic Party--Cox
Trying to carry on Wilson's plea for support to the League of Nations.

610. Riches and reform. (DAP 331)
1920--Democratic Party--Cox
A Tammany Hall slogan invented by Charles F. Murphy. Meant to be a gibe against reformers.

611. Harding, You're the Man for Us. (F 108)
1920--Republican Party--Harding
Title of a popular song by Al Jolson.

612. Happy Hooligan. (B 231)
1920--Democratic Party--Cox
James Cox likened Warren Harding to the comic strip character.

613. Back to Normalcy. (LO 556; BAR 76; B 762; BO 230; M 193)
1920--Republican Party--Harding
From a speech by Harding in which he created a

new word which became the keyword of the campaign.

614. Restore all power to the people. (J 224)
    1920--Farmer-Labor Party--Christensen
    From the preamble to the party platform.

615. To stabilize America First / To safeguard America
    First / To prosper America First / To think of
    America First / To exalt America First / To live
    for and revere America First. (M 193)
    1920--Republican Party--Harding
    From a campaign speech given by Harding before
    the Ohio Society in N. Y. City.

616. Thrift and industry. (S 2375)
    1920--Republican Party--Harding
    The slogan which became identified with Vice-
    Presidential candidate Coolidge.

617. Let's be done with wiggle and wobble. (B 762;
    S 2371)
    1920--Republican Party--Harding
    Harding had a gift for colorful phrases.

618. America First. (F 107)
    1920--Democratic Party--Cox
    From a campaign banner.

619. Coolidge or Chaos. (BAR 134)
    1920--Republican Party--Coolidge
    Republicans emphasized stability. This slogan was
    their reply to the Democratic platform (see en-
    try no. 626).

620. Keep Cool and Keep Coolidge. (BO 234)
    1924--Republican Party--Coolidge
    Republican campaign slogans used various plays on
    Coolidge's name.

621. Keep Cool with Coolidge. (S 2466)
    1924--Republican Party--Coolidge

622. We must wage a new war for freedom. (J 255)
    1924--Progressive Party--LaFollette
    From the Party platform.

623. Honesty at Home--Honor Abroad. (B 795)
     1924--Democratic Party--Davis
     The Democratic Party was denouncing Republican
     corruption, especially the Teapot Dome scandal.

624. Silent Cal. (BO 234)
     1924--Republican Party--Coolidge
     The Republicans made a virtue of Coolidge's taci-
     turnity.

625. A vote for Coolidge is a vote for chaos. (J 244;
     LO 570)
     1924--Democratic Party--Davis
     A reference to Republican corruption; from the
     party platform.

626. Equal rights to all and special privilege to none.
     (J 243)
     1924--Democratic Party--Davis
     From the party platform.

627. Cautious Cal and Charging Charlie. (LO 566)
     1924--Republican Party--Coolidge
     A slogan contrasting the styles of Presidential
     candidate Calvin Coolidge and Vice-Presidential
     candidate Charles Dawes.

628. Down with injunctions and the use of Police and Sol-
     diers against Workers. (J 269)
     1924--Workers Party--William Z. Foster
     From the party platform.

629. The nation may grow rich in the vision of greed /
     The nation will grow great in the vision of service.
     (J 256)
     1924--Progressive Party--LaFollette
     From the party platform.

630. Down with Militarism and Imperialist Wars. (J 269)
     1924--Workers Party--Foster
     From the party platform.

631. Remember the Teapot Dome. (B 795)
     1924--Democratic Party--Davis
     A slogan recalling the corrupt deals at Teapot
     Dome, Wyoming by some of Harding's close
     advisors.

632.   The business of America is business.   (DU 243)
         1924--Republican Party--Coolidge
         Coolidge was emphasizing his solid conservatism
            contrasted to Harding's playboy image.

633.   Release all Political and Class War Prisoners.
         (J 269)
         1924--Workers Party--Foster
         From the party platform.

634.   Rugged Individualism.   (L 375; B 805)
         1928--Republican Party--Hoover
         A slogan which recurred throughout Hoover's ad-
            ministration.

635.   Honest, Able, Fearless.   (F 113)
         1928--Democratic Party--Alfred E. Smith
         A campaign poster.

636.   Rum, Romanism and Tammany.   (F 114)
         1928--Republican Party--Hoover
         An attack on Al Smith's Catholicism, his anti-
            Prohibition stand, and his association with Tam-
            many Hall.

637.   On to Washington.   (F 115)
         1928--Democratic Party--Smith
         Popular banner in purple, yellow, red, white, and
            blue.

638.   A Vote for Al Smith Is a Vote for the Pope.   (B 805)
         1928--Republican Party--Hoover
         Anti-Catholic sentiment (as well as a resurgence
            of the Klan) was abundantly evident in this cam-
            paign.   Al Smith was the first Catholic presi-
            dential candidate.

639.   The "Great Engineer."   (BO 251)
         1928--Republican Party--Hoover
         Hoover's professional experience was promoted as
            indicating his ability to run the country efficiently.

640.   Happy Warrior.   (BAR 137; LO 574)
         1928--Democratic Party--Smith
         Smith was nominated by Franklin Delano Roosevelt
            as a man of determination and success--"the
            happy warrior."

641. A chicken (or two chickens) in every pot and two cars in every garage. (JO 8; B 805; BAR 76; LO 583)
    1928--Republican Party--Hoover
    The Republicans promised continued prosperity--a promise they bitterly regretted.

642. Let's look at the record. (LO 583)
    1928--Democratic Party--Smith
    Smith's frequently repeated phrase during the campaign became a catchword.

643. Let's keep what we've got--Prosperity didn't just happen. (LO 578)
    1928--Republican Party--Hoover
    Another reference to the prosperous twenties.

644. Rum-soaked Romanist. (LO 579)
    1928--Republican Party--Hoover
    Al Smith's Catholicism and anti-Prohibition stance.

645. I do not choose to run. (LO 574)
    1928--Republican Party--Hoover
    Republicans fully expected Coolidge to be their nominee until he called a press conference on August 2, 1927, and gave reporters copies of his succinct hand-written note.

646. The watchword of the day should be: "Turn the rascals out." (J 271)
    1928--Democratic Party--Smith
    From the party platform (see entry no. 356).

647. Everybody Ought to Be Rich. (M 268)
    1928--Democratic Party--Smith
    John J. Rascob's magazine article with this title was picked up as a campaign slogan.

648. Down with capitalist rule! (J 324)
    1928--Workers (Communist) Party--Foster
    From the party platform.

649. Not a man, not a gun, not a cent for the imperialist army and navy. (J 309)
    1928--Workers (Communist) Party--Foster
    From the party platform.

650. Forward to a Workers' and Farmers' Government! (J 324)

1928--Workers (Communist) Party--Foster
Party platform.

651. Hands off Mexico!   (J 309)
1928--Workers (Communist) Party--Foster
In 1926 war with Mexico over United States business interests seemed imminent although "Cool
Cal's" appointment of Ambassador Dwight Mor-
row and a Senate resolution for arbitration had
cooled the situation.

652. Down with the imperialist war against Nicaragua!
(J 309)
1928--Workers (Communist) Party--Foster
Coolidge had sent 2,000 Marines into Nicaragua
against guerrilla general Augusto Sandino.

653. Rally around the platform of the class struggle!
(J 324)
1928--Workers (Communist) Party--Foster

654. Is your bread buttered?   (S 2607)
1928--Republican Party--Hoover
The prosperity theme again.

655. Let's keep what we've got.   (S 2607)
1928--Republican Party--Hoover
--and again.

656. We offer not promises but accomplishments.   (J 281)
1928--Republican Party--Hoover
From the party platform.

657. Forward with Roosevelt--No Retreat.   (F 120)
1932--Democratic Party--Roosevelt
An automobile license plate attachment.

658. Brother, can you spare a dime?   (Z 381)
1932--Democratic Party--Roosevelt
A Yip Harburg song used as a Democratic remind-
er of the Depression.

659. Bread, Butter, Bacon, and Beans.   (S 2724)
1932--Democratic Party--Roosevelt
A slogan from the Democratic Convention by supporters of William "Alfalfa" Murray, a con-
tender for the nomination.

660. Hoover cleaned us all. (JO 14)
    1932--Democratic Party--Roosevelt
    The deepening Depression was an overriding cam-
    paign theme as illustrated by this reference to
    a well-known vacuum cleaner.

661. Share the wealth. (DAP 343)
    1932--Democratic Party--Roosevelt
    A quote from FDR's acceptance speech, used again
    by Huey Long.

662. Good Neighbor Policy. (DAP 175; B 830; JO 106)
    1932--Democratic Party--Roosevelt
    From Roosevelt's inaugural address on March 4,
    1933.

663. Welcome to Roosevelt from the Forgotten Man.
    (JO 44)
    1932--Democratic Party--Roosevelt
    From a banner welcoming Roosevelt to Los Angeles
    during his campaign. The "forgotten man" be-
    came a key term (see entry no. 680).

664. New Deal. (LO 606; BO 259; BAR 245; JO 44)
    1932--Democratic Party--Roosevelt
    From Roosevelt's acceptance speech at the Conven-
    tion: "I pledge myself to a new deal for the
    American people" (a quote from Mark Twain's
    Connecticut Yankee).

665. Heroes in 1917--Bums in 1932. (JO 37)
    1932--Democratic Party--Roosevelt
    A slogan of World War I veterans, unemployed
    during the Depression, some of whom had been
    among the Bonus Marchers who were dispersed
    by the Army on Hoover's orders.

666. Billions for Bankers--Bullets for Vets. (JO 37)
    1932--Democratic Party--Roosevelt
    Another reference to the Bonus Marchers.

667. Down with Hoover, Slayer of Veterans. (JO 37)
    1932--Democratic Party--Roosevelt
    Hoover paid dearly for using the Army against
    unemployed veterans.

668. A gallant leader. (F 122)

1932--Democratic Party--Roosevelt
A campaign poster.

669. In Hoover We Trusted; / Now We Are Busted. (JO 36)
1932--Democratic Party--Roosevelt
This slogan came from bankrupt Iowan farmers.

670. We Want Living Prices, Not Credit. (JO 36)
1932--Democratic Party--Roosevelt
Another Iowan farm slogan.

671. Hoover, Hyde, Hell and Hard Times-- / The Republican 4H Club. (JO 36)
1932--Democratic Party--Roosevelt
Farmers who had been hard hit by the Depression were especially bitter against Hoover and Hyde, his Secretary of Agriculture, for their farm policies.

672. Hoover's Record: Millions for Bankers--Hunger for Workers. (JO 37)
1932--Democratic Party--Roosevelt
From a campaign banner used in Detroit.

673. Brain Trust. (DAP 44)
1932--Democratic Party--Roosevelt
The nickname for the group of academics and intellectuals who advised Roosevelt during the campaign and after.

674. Happy Days Are Here Again. (BAR 244; M 366; BO 253; LO 592)
1932--Democratic Party--Roosevelt
Roosevelt's theme song from the Convention when Senator George Norris announced his support for Roosevelt and throughout the campaign and his first Administration.

675. Destruction, Delay, Deceit, Despair. (BAR 246)
1932--Democratic Party--Roosevelt
Roosevelt's characterization of his opponents.

676. Everything Will Be Rosy with Roosevelt. (B 832)
1932--Democratic Party--Roosevelt

677. Prosperity Is Just Around the Corner. (LO 597; B 832)

1932--Republican Party--Hoover
A persistent theme of the Republicans from 1929
through the end of the 1932 campaign.

678.   The Worst Is Past.   (B 832)
1932--Republican Party--Hoover
A variation of entry no. 677.

679.   If You are Wet, Vote for Smith, If You are Dry, /
Vote for Garner, If You Don't Know What You Are, /
Vote for Roosevelt.   (M 299)
1932--Democratic Party--Roosevelt
Al Smith and John Nance Garner were both contend-
ers for the nomination.

680.   Forgotten Man.   (LO 592; M 290)
1932--Democratic Party--Roosevelt
From a speech delivered by Roosevelt on April 7,
1932.   Speech-writer Raymond Moley was quot-
ing William Graham Sumner.

681.   Grass will grow in the streets of a hundred cities.
(LO 598)
1932--Republican Party--Hoover
A prediction of what would happen if Roosevelt
should be elected.

682.   For a United States of Soviet America.   (J 330;
S 2731)
1932--Communist Party--Foster
From the party platform.

683.   Rally Against Starvation and War.   (J 330)
1932--Communist Party--Foster
From the party platform.

684.   Justice, peace and freedom.   (J 351)
1932--Socialist Party--Thomas
From the party platform.

685.   Equal rights to all; special privilege to none.   (J 333)
1932--Democratic Party--Roosevelt
From the party platform.   (See entry no. 626.)

686.   We Do Our Part.   (J 68)
1933--Roosevelt
The NRA (National Recovery Act) slogan.   (A Los

Angeles barbershop variation read: We do our
part, we do our part / We do our haircut, too
/ And we display our art / In every oil sham-
poo.)

687. Jew Deal. (MO, v3, 325)
    1934--Charles E. Coughlin
    Fr. Coughlin, head of the Shrine of the Little
        Flower in Detroit, first supported, then broke
        with Roosevelt. A notorious anti-Semite, this
        was his version of the New Deal.

688. $200 a month for life. (MO, v3, 325)
    1934--Francis E. Townsend
    Author of the "Townsend Plan," he put forward
        various proposals for pensions for seniors.

689. $60 at 60. (Oakland, Calif. Museum Exhibit)
    1934--Francis E. Townsend
    Dr. Townsend proposed senior pensions.

690. Thirty dollars every Thursday. (Oakland, Calif.
    Museum Exhibit)
    1934--Francis E. Townsend
    Another pension proposal.

691. End Poverty In California. (MO, v3, 325)
    1934--Upton Sinclair
    Sinclair ran for Governor of California with this
        slogan--EPIC, for short.

692. Every Man a King. (MO, v3, 326; JO 85)
    1935--Huey Long
    Nicknamed "The Kingfish," Long announced him-
        self as a candidate for President but was as-
        sassinated.

693. Share Our Wealth. (MO, v3, 326; JO 85)
    1935--Huey Long
    Long proposed this slogan for his campaign, cut
        short by his assassination. It had earlier been
        used by FDR in 1932 (see entry no. 661).

694. Keep the People's Heart in Government. (F 126)
    1936--Democratic Party--Roosevelt
    Slogan on a give-away fan, one of the campaign
        devices.

695. Roosevelt and Humanity. (F 126)
1936--Democratic Party--Roosevelt
Used during FDR's second bid for the Presidency.

696. Carry On with Roosevelt. (F 125)
1936--Democratic Party--Roosevelt
From a campaign banner.

697. Let America Be America Again. (Z 395)
1936--Democratic Party--Roosevelt
From a Langston Hughes poem.

698. Communism Is Twentieth Century Americanism.
(J 360; L 450)
1936--Communist Party--Browder
From the party platform.

699. Landon, oh, Landon / Will lead to victory / With the
dear old Constitution / And it's good enough for me.
(LO 613)
1936--Republican Party--Alfred Landon
A campaign jingle.

700. Life, Liberty and Landon. (LO 620)
1936--Republican Party--Landon
Landon's campaign slogan. His symbol was the
sunflower.

701. Three hard years with Hoover / Three good years
with Roosevelt. (LOR 606)
1936--Democratic Party--Roosevelt
Chanted by Roosevelt supporters at the 1936 Convention.

702. The More Abundant Life. (S 2817)
1936--Republican Party--Landon

703. Security, plenty, peace and freedom. (J 370)
1936--Socialist Party--Thomas
From the party platform.

704. Rendezvous with Destiny. (BAR 253)
1936--Democratic Party--Roosevelt
From FDR's acceptance speech at the Convention.

705. Remember Hoover! (B 849)
1936--Democratic Party--Roosevelt

706. Let's Get Another Deck. (B 849)
     1936--Republican Party--Landon

707. Save the American Way of Life. (MO, v3, 328)
     1936--Republican Party--Landon

708. As Maine goes, so goes Vermont. (MO, v3, 328)
     1936--Democratic Party--Roosevelt
     A quip by James Farley, who changed the old say-
     ing "As goes Maine, so goes the nation" to re-
     flect the election results. Maine and Vermont
     were the only states Landon carried.

709. Defeat the New Deal and Its Reckless Spending.
     (B 849)
     1936--Republican Party--Landon
     One of the objections to Roosevelt's economic pro-
     gram was its cost in federal funding.

710. Put America Back to Work (J 357)
     1936--Communist Party--Browder
     From the Party platform.

711. Share the Wealth. (DAP 385)
     1936--Union Party--Lemke
     Lemke used the slogan originally used by FDR and
     then again by Huey Long (see entry nos. 661
     and 693).

712. Collective Security Against Fascist Aggression.
     (J 116)
     1936--Communist Party--Browder
     From the party platform (see entry no. 730).

713. Economic Royalists. (B 849; JO 89)
     1936--Democratic Party--Roosevelt
     From FDR's acceptance speech on June 27, 1936:
     "These economic royalists ... really complain
     that we seek to take away their power. "

714. That Man in the White House. (JO 87)
     1936--Republican Party--Landon
     Republicans referred to Roosevelt with loathing.
     The phrase was picked up by cartoonists, news-
     paper columnists, etc.

715. Free enterprise, private competition and equality of

opportunity.   (MO, v3, 328)
    1936--Republican Party--Landon
    From the party platform.

716. That Madman in the White House.   (MO, v3, 329)
    1936--Republican Party--Landon
    Opposition to FDR became virulent by his second administration.

717. A traitor to his class.   (MO, v3, 329)
    1936--Republican Party--Landon
    Big business opposition to Roosevelt led to this characterization.

718. Forward to a progressive, free, prosperous and happy America / VOTE COMMUNIST!   (J 360)
    1936--Communist Party--Browder
    From the party platform.

719. Democracy or Fascism, Progress or Reaction. (J 357)
    1936--Communist Party--Browder
    From the party platform.

720. Peace, freedom, and the security of the people. (J 357)
    1936--Communist Party--Browder
    From the party platform.

721. Keep America Out of War by Keeping War Out of the World.   (J 359)
    1936--Communist Party--Browder
    From the party platform.

722. No one can be sure.   (S 2818)
    1936--Republican Party--Landon
    From Landon's Madison Square Garden speech.

723. America shall be self-contained and self-sustained. (J 375; S 2864)
    1936--Union Party--Lemke

724. I'm tired, oh, so tired of the Whole New Deal / Of the juggler's smile and the barker's spiel / Of the mushy speech and the loud bassoon / And tiredest of all of our leader's croon.   (S 2819)
    1936--Republican Party--Landon

This campaign jingle was read into the <u>Congressional Record</u>.

725. Cash and carry. (DAP 54; L 474)
1937--Roosevelt
As part of the neutrality policy of the United States the President could require belligerents who purchased non-military goods from the United States to pay cash and to use their own ships.

726. Quarantine the Aggressor. (MO, v3, 347; L 475)
1937--Roosevelt
From a speech by FDR in Chicago.

727. Four Horsemen. (L 421; LOR 615)
1937--Roosevelt
When the Supreme Court invalidated some New Deal legislation, FDR attacked especially four of the conservative Justices: James McReynolds, George Sutherland, Willis Van Devanter, and Pierce Butler.

728. Nine Old Men. (B 850; DAP 264)
1937--Roosevelt
The conservative Supreme Court, all appointed by his predecessors, was attacked by FDR, who proposed to "pack" the Court with additional appointments.

729. One third of a nation ill-housed, ill-clad, ill-nourished. (L 424)
1937--Roosevelt
From his annual message to Congress.

730. Collective security against aggression. (S 2926)
1938--Roosevelt
(See entry no. 712.)

731. Non-belligerent, but not neutral. (H 479)
1939--Roosevelt
Roosevelt's response to the beginning of the war in Europe.

732. Again, and again, and again. (LO 646; S 2944)
1940--Democratic Party--Roosevelt
From a speech by FDR on October 30 in Boston during which he reassured Americans: "I shall

say it again, and again, and again. Your boys
are not going to be sent into any foreign wars. "

733. I roll my own. (S 2938)
    1940--Republican Party--Willkie
    Willkie's reply when asked who wrote his speeches.

734. To Keep the Nation Firm / Give Him Another Term.
    (F 130)
    1940--Democratic Party--Roosevelt
    From a banner. Roosevelt was trying for an un-
    precedented third term.

735. Eleanor start packing, the Willkies Are Coming.
    (F 131)
    1940--Republican Party--Willkie
    From a campaign button.

736. The spirit of the common man is the spirit of peace
    and goodwill. (BAR 159)
    1940--Democratic Party--Roosevelt

737. Better a Third Term than a Third-Rater. (B 872)
    1940--Democratic Party--Roosevelt
    The third-term issue was a hot one in 1940.

738. There's No Indispensable Man. (B 872)
    1940--Republican Party--Willkie
    Both Democrats and Republicans debated the third-
    term issue.

739. Two Good Terms Deserve Another. (LO 653)
    1940--Democratic Party--Roosevelt

740. Two Good Terms Deserve a Rest. (F 131; LO 628)
    1940--Republican Party--Willkie

741. Martin, Barton and Fish. (LO 647; JO 136)
    1940--Democratic Party--Roosevelt
    Roosevelt attacked the conservative triumvirate in
    Congress--Joseph Martin, Bruce Barton and
    Hamilton Fish--in a speech on October 28, 1940.

742. Arsenal of Democracy. (L 493; DAP 25)
    1940--Democratic Party--Roosevelt
    In one of his "fireside chats" on December 29,
    1940, FDR said, "We must become the great
    arsenal of democracy. "

743. Willkie for President--of Commonwealth & Southern.
(LO 653)
   1940--Democratic Party--Roosevelt
   Willkie was an executive of a utility company and
   a corporation lawyer.

744. Freedom, Democracy, Roosevelt. (F 130)
   1940--Democratic Party--Roosevelt
   From an automobile license plate holder.

745. We don't want Eleanor either. (F 131; LO 653)
   1940--Republican Party--Willkie
   A campaign button.

746. Not a cent, not a gun, not a man for war preparations
and imperialist war. (LO 653)
   1940--Communist Party--Browder
   From the party platform.

747. Americanism, preparedness and peace. (LO 636)
   1940--Republican Party--Willkie

748. We want Willkie. (LO 637)
   1940--Republican Party--Willkie
   Beginning as a chant at the Convention, this slo-
      gan blossomed on buttons, posters, banners,
      leaflets and automobile bumper stickers.

749. Win with Willkie. (BAR 143; LO 635)
   1940--Republican Party--Willkie
   Another popular slogan on buttons and posters.

750. The simple, barefoot Wall Street lawyer. (LO 628)
   1940--Democratic Party--Roosevelt
   An attack by Harold Ickes on Willkie's pretensions
      to being a "common man" rather than the cor-
      poration lawyer he was.

751. Franklin Delano Roosevelt / Fairly Deserves Re-
election. (Oakland, Calif. Musuem Exhibit)
   1940--Democratic Party--Roosevelt

752. No More Fireside Chats. (LO 628)
   1940--Republican Party--Willkie
   Roosevelt had made his radio "fireside chats" into
      a popular method for communicating with the
      public and for explaining his policies.

753. Dictator? Not for US. (LO 628)
     1940--Republican Party--Willkie
     Roosevelt was accused of wanting to become a
         dictator.

754. Give Roosevelt His Desired Rest. (F 131; LO 628)
     1940--Republican Party--Willkie
     From a campaign button.

755. No New Deal--We Want a Square Deal. (LO 628)
     1940--Republican Party--Willkie
     Willkie was harking back to Teddy Roosevelt's
         1904 slogan.

756. Force Franklin Out at Third. (F 131; LO 628)
     1940--Republican Party--Willkie
     From a campaign button. Another reference to
         the third-term issue (and to baseball).

757. No third term. (LO 628)
     1940--Republican Party--Willkie

758. No Franklin the First. (F 131; LO 628)
     1940--Republican Party--Willkie
     A campaign button.

759. We Must Strengthen Democracy. (J 382)
     1940--Democratic Party--Roosevelt
     From the party platform.

760. Keep America Out of War! (J 399)
     1940--Socialist Party--Thomas
     From the party platform.

761. The Workshops to the Workers! / The Product to the
     Producers! / All Power to the Socialist Industrial
     Union! (J 401)
         1940--Socialist Labor Party--Aikin
         From the party platform.

762. Bring on the Champ! (A 573)
     1940--Republican Party--Willkie
     A sports metaphor.

763. A vote for the Communist Party is a vote against im-
     perialist war. (J 381)
         1940--Communist Party--Browder

In 1940 the Communist Party characterized the war
in Europe as imperialist. In June 1941, when
Hitler invaded the Soviet Union, their position
changed.

764.   Full Rights for the Negro People! (J 379)
       1940--Communist Party--Browder
       From the party platform.

765.   Keep America Out of the Imperialist War. (J 379)
       1940--Communist Party--Browder
       Another verion of entry no. 763.

766.   For a People's Peace. (J 379)
       1940--Communist Party--Browder

767.   America First. (L 487)
       1940--Liberty League
       Isolationists and non-interventionists from both
          parties offered this slogan used earlier in 1920
          (see entry no. 618).

768.   The Faith That Is America. (BAR 108)
       1940--Republican Party--Willkie

769.   Our "American Faith." (BAR 158)
       1940--Republican Party--Willkie
       Another verion of entry no. 768.

770.   Crusade to Preserve American Democracy. (BAR 158)
       1940--Republican Party--Willkie
       Republicans warned that Roosevelt's policies had
          been sapping fundamental democratic institutions
          and principles.

771.   The New Fear. (BAR 143)
       1940--Republican Party--Willkie
       The fear that democracy was being eroded and
          that the United States would be embroiled in the
          war in Europe.

772a. Britain Is Fighting Our Fight
    b. The Yanks Are Not Coming
    c. England Will Fight to the Last American
    d. All Methods Short of War
    e. Lend-Lease
       Slogans popular in the United States during World

War II (before December 7, 1941). From songs, banners, posters, films of the period.

773a. Get Hirohito first!
    b. Yellow-bellied Japs
    c. Praise the Lord and Pass the Ammunition
    d. Unconditional surrender
    e. Remember Pearl Harbor
    f. A day which will live in infamy
        Slogans popular in the United States during World War II (after December 7, 1941). From songs, banners, posters, films of the period.

774. Century of the Common Man. (LO 657; JO 163)
      1942--Henry Wallace
      From a speech by Vice-President Henry Wallace on May 8, 1942. The phrase was used in post-war campaigns.

775. America Wants Dewey. (LOR 652)
      1944--Republican Party--Dewey
      Slogan on Convention posters.

776. Roosevelt and a lasting peace. (LOR 656)
      1944--Democratic Party--Roosevelt
      Slogan on Convention posters.

777. I want you, FDR. / Stay and finish the job. (F 134)
      1944--Democratic Party--Roosevelt
      From a campaign poster.

778. Let's Re-Re-Re-Elect Roosevelt. (F 135)
      1944--Democratic Party--Roosevelt
      From a campaign song reflecting support for a fourth term.

779. The difference between Democrats and Republicans is 12 Years Experience. (F 136)
      1944--Democratic Party--Roosevelt
      From a campaign poster.

780. People's War Against Fascism. (Z 398)
      1944--Communist Party
      The Communist characterization of the war changed on June 22, 1941 (see entry no. 763).

781. One man government. (S 3036)

1944--Republican Party--Dewey
Dewey accused Roosevelt of desiring to be a despot.

782. Pay as you go tax plan. (S 3013)
1944--Democratic Party--Roosevelt
A proposal for a withholding tax (authored by economist Beardsley Ruml) was defeated in Congress.

783. Again and again and again. (LO 671)
1944--Democratic Party--Roosevelt
In a campaign speech defending his action during the war, Roosevelt used once more the phrase which had become a slogan in 1940 (see entry no. 732).

784. Tired old man. (LO 662)
1944--Republican Party--Dewey
Dewey was alluding to Roosevelt's age and illness.

785. Sidney Hillman and Earl Browder's Communists have registered. Have you? (S 3034)
1944--Republican Party--Dewey
Dewey harped repeatedly on Communist and labor influence on Roosevelt. Earl Browder was head of the Communist Party and Sidney Hillman the head of the Congress of Industrial Organization (CIO).

786. Destroy the Browder-Hillman Axis. (S 3034)
1944--Republican Party--Dewey
A play on the Hitler-Mussolini-Hirohito Axis.

787. It's your country. Why let Sidney Hillman run it? Vote for Dewey and Bricker. (LO 676)
1944--Republican Party--Dewey
Sidney Hillman, head of the CIO, was accused by the Republicans of exerting undue influence on Roosevelt.

788. Clear it with Sidney. (LO 660; JO 167)
1944--Republican Party--Dewey
Roosevelt had sought the approval of Sidney Hillman, influential labor leader of the CIO, in making the final choice of the Democratic Vice-Presidential candidate.

789. Clear Everything with Sidney. (S 3034)

1944--Republican Party--Dewey
Another version of entry no. 788.

790. Speed victory, establish and maintain peace, guarantee full employment and provide prosperity. (J 402)
1944--Democratic Party--Roosevelt
From the party platform.

791. Brotherhood of man, Peace, Plenty and International Fraternity. (J 418)
1944--Socialist Labor Party--Teichert
From the party platform.

792. Cold War. (DAP 72)
1946--Truman
A phrase for postwar tensions between the United States and the Soviet Union.

793. Truman Doctrine. (MO, v3, 424)
1947--Truman
From Truman's Message to Congress on March 12, 1947, which proposed that the United States defend countries anywhere resisting "subjugation by armed minorities or outside pressures."

794. Marshall Plan. (MO, v3, 423; DAP 238)
1947--Truman
Proposed by Secretary of State Marshall for the United States to provide financial aid for the reconstruction of war-devastated countries.

795. Give 'em hell, Harry. (LO 713; JO 233)
1948--Democratic Party--Truman
A quote from Truman's comment: "I'm going to fight hard; I'm going to give 'em hell."

796. Fair Deal. (L 680; BO 281; DAP 146; LO 734)
1948--Democratic Party--Truman
Truman's successor to Teddy's Square Deal and FDR's New Deal.

797. Had Enough? (JO 226)
1948--Republican Party--Dewey
Republicans hoped for success after 16 years of Democratic administrations.

798. Harry, Henry, Dewey--Phooey! (LO 721)

1948--States' Rights Party--Thurmond
Strom Thurmond opposed all the other candidates--
Harry Truman, Henry Wallace and Thomas
Dewey--in his right-wing breakaway from the
Democratic Party.

799. Get right with Thurmond and Wright. (LO 721)
1948--States' Rights Party--Thurmond
Governor Fielding Wright of Mississippi was Thurmond's running mate on the "Dixiecrat" ticket.

800. I'm just wild about Harry. (BO 282)
1948--Democratic Party--Truman
Posters and buttons proclaimed this slogan widely.

801. Bosses, boodle, buncombe and blarney. (LOR 684)
1948--Republican Party--Dewey
From the Convention keynote speech by Governor
Dwight Green of Illinois referring to the Democratic Party.

802. Rule by the moneybaggers. (S 3127)
1948--Democratic Party--Truman
Truman attacked the Republicans as representative
of the rich only.

803. Peace, Freedom and Abundance. (S 3121)
1948--Progressive Party--Wallace
The left-wing breakaway from the Democratic
Party.

804. The party of special interests. (S 3119)
1948--Democratic Party--Truman
Truman's attack on the Republican Party.

805. Dixiecrats. (DAP 124)
1948--States Rights Party--Thurmond
Nickname for the Southern Democrats who broke
with the Party at the 1948 Convention.

806. Not peace in our time but peace for all time. (LO
711)
1948--Democratic Party--Truman
A hope rather than a promise.

807. Save What's Left. (B 920)
1948--Republican Party--Dewey

Republicans accused the Democrats of mismanagement.

808. That no-account, do-nothing, Republican 80th Congress. (BAR 57; LOR 685)
      1948--Democratic Party--Truman
      Truman attacked the 80th Congress in his campaign speeches.

809. God and our native land. (J 419)
      1948--Christian Nationalist Party--Smith
      From the party platform.

810. To serve the interests of all and not the few. (J 431)
      1948--Democratic Party--Truman
      From the party platform.

811. Never before have so few owned so much at the expense of so many. (J 437)
      1948--Progressive Party--Wallace
      From the party platform.

812. Capitalist Despotism or Socialist Freedom. (J 461)
      1948--Socialist Labor Party--Teichert
      From the party platform.

813. Liberty, opportunity and justice for all. (J 450)
      1948--Republican Party--Dewey
      From the party platform.

814. You never had it so good. (S 3248; B 932; LO 772)
      1952--Democratic Party--Stevenson
      The Democrats campaigned on continued prosperity under Democratic administrations.

815. I will (shall) go to Korea. (BAR 269; JO 259; LO 765)
      1952--Republican Party--Eisenhower
      Eisenhower pledged to go personally to Korea to negotiate an end to the war.

816. The Middle Road. (LO 758)
      1952--Republican Party--Eisenhower
      The Republicans claimed they had avoided extremes either on the right or the left. They implied the Democrats were buffeted by both extremes.

817. Corruption in high places. (LO 749)

1952--Republican Party--Eisenhower
Republicans charged that officials in the Truman
Administration had accepted bribes from lobby-
ists.

818. K_1 C_2. (LO 740)
1952--Republican Party--Eisenhower
The cryptic slogan stood for "Korea, Communism
and Corruption," evils charged to the Democrats.

819. I like Ike. (LO 758; BO 290)
1952--Republican Party--Eisenhower
Millions of campaign buttons popularized Eisenhower's nickname.

820. Ben Hogan for President, If We're Going to Have a
Golfer, / Let's Have a Good One. (BO 297)
1952--Democratic Party--Stevenson
Bumpersticker critical of Eisenhower's penchant
for golf.

821. Appeasement of Communism / At home and abroad.
(JO 256)
1952--Republican Party--Eisenhower
Charges against the Truman Administration.

822. Fair Play. (JO 250)
1952--Republican Party--Eisenhower
Eisenhower's pledge to the voters.

823. Peace with Honor. (J 474)
1952--Democratic Party--Stevenson
From the party platform.

824. A new and better day. (J 505)
1952--Republican Party--Eisenhower
From the party platform.

825. Free industrial government for all mankind. (J 566)
1952--Socialist Labor Party--Hass
From the party platform.

826. For a Workers and Farmers Government. (J 522)
1952--Socialist Workers Party--Dobbs
From the party platform.

827. Restore the Bill of Rights to All Americans.   (J 489)
     1952--Progressive Party--Hallinan
     From the party platform.

828. Full and Equal Rights for the Negro People--Now.
     (J 489)
     1952--Progressive Party--Hallinan
     From the party platform.

829. Cease Fire in Korea at Once / No Ifs, Ands or Buts.
     (J 487)
     1952--Progressive Party--Hallinan
     Vincent Hallinan, candidate for President, cam-
     paigned on this issue from party platform.

830. The Socialist objective: Humanity First.   (J 515)
     1952--Socialist Party--Hoopes
     From the party platform.

831. Ike and Mamie--The People's Future / Is with You in
     '52.   (DU 287)
     1952--Republican Party--Eisenhower
     A campaign banner.

832. Dynamic conservatism.   (DU 293)
     1952--Republican Party--Eisenhower
     Eisenhower's own characterization of his Adminis-
     tration.

833. Had Enough?   (B 933)
     1952--Republican Party--Eisenhower
     Republicans stressed that 20 years of Democratic
     Administrations were enough.

834. Elect Men You Can Trust.   (Election poster, Oakland,
     Calif. Museum)
     1952--Republican Party--Eisenhower
     Another thrust at corruption in the Truman ranks.

835. Time for a Change.   (BAR 76; LO 758; S 3251)
     1952--Republican Party--Eisenhower

836. The Mess in Washington.   (LO 740; DU 288; BAR 110;
     S 3251)
     1952--Republican Party--Eisenhower
     Stevenson, the Democratic candidate, originated the

phrase, but it was turned into a campaign slogan by Republicans.

837. Eisenhower--Nixon / They're for You! (Election handbill, Oakland, Calif. Museum)
1952--Republican Party--Eisenhower

838. A respectable Republican cloth coat. (LO 765; S 3321)
1952--Republican Party--Eisenhower
From Vice-Presidential candidate, Richard Nixon's "Checkers" speech of September 23, 1952. Democrats also used the phrase--ironically as a campaign slogan against the Republicans.

839. Crime, corruption, Communism, Korea. (BAR 269; S 3352)
1952--Republican Party--Eisenhower
The Republican Party's charges against the Truman Administration.

840. Twenty years of treason. (L 746)
1952--Republican Party--Eisenhower
The accusation Senator Joseph McCarthy hurled at previous Democratic Administrations.

841. Great Crusade. (LO 760; S 3241)
1952--Republican Party--Eisenhower

842. Soft on Communism. (S 3221)
1952--Republican Party--Eisenhower
Senator McCarthy and Senator Taft charged the Democrats with failure to challenge Communism strongly.

843. Adlai the Appeaser. (BO 269)
1952--Republican Party--Eisenhower
Nixon, Eisenhower's running mate, coined this epithet.

844. America Needs Stevenson. (F 142)
1952--Democratic Party--Stevenson
Banners at the Democratic Convention.

845. All the way with Adlai. (LO 800)
1956--Democratic Party--Stevenson

846. Peace, Progress, Prosperity. (BAR 284; LO 798)
1956--Republican Party--Eisenhower

847. There must be no second-class citizens in this country. (MO, v3, 458)
     1956--Republican Party--Eisenhower

848. For the return of America to the highway of progress.
(J 524)
     1956--Democratic Party--Stevenson
     From the party platform.

849. Modern Republicanism. (JO 279)
     1956--Republican Party--Eisenhower

850. A New America. (LO 790)
     1956--Democratic Party--Stevenson

851. For a Brighter Tomorrow. (J 561)
     1956--Republican Party--Eisenhower
     From the party platform.

852. Tax the rich, not the poor. (J 573)
     1956--Socialist Workers Party--Dobbs

853. Socialism Will Cleanse Society. (J 573)
     1956--Socialist Labor Party--Hass

854. Talk sense to the American people. (C 7)
     1956--Democratic Party--Stevenson

855. A part-time leader. (S 3350)
     1956--Democratic Party--Stevenson
     Stevenson's attack on Eisenhower for his frequent
        vacations, golf games, and illnesses.

856. Get America moving again. (BAR 283)
     1956--Democratic Party--Stevenson

857. Without freedom there is no true socialism and without socialism there can be no enduring freedom.
(J 562)
     1956--Socialist Party--Hoopes
     From the party platform.

858. Man of the 60's. (F 152)
     1960--Democratic Party--Kennedy
     From a campaign handout.

859. Kennedy is the remedy. (F 154)

1960--Democratic Party--Kennedy
A badge on a campaign vest.

860. New Frontier. (LO 823; BO 301; Z 562)
1960--Democratic Party--Kennedy
Key slogan of the campaign.

861. Win with Jack. (F 155)
1960--Democratic Party--Kennedy

862. The party of hope and the party of memory. (J 600)
1960--Democratic Party--Kennedy
The Democratic Party platform characterized itself
as the party of the future and the Republican
Party as looking to the past.

863. There is no price ceiling on America's security.
(J 608)
1960--Republican Party--Nixon
From the party platform.

864. Socialism and Survival vs. Capitalism and Catastrophe.
(J 634)
1960--Socialist Labor Party--Hass

865. Tricky Dick. (LO 838)
1960--Democratic Party--Kennedy
Revived in 1960, a nickname for Nixon dating back
to his 1956 campaign for Vice-President and
accusations of building a secret "slush fund."

866. Put America first. (LO 846)
1960--Republican Party--Nixon

867. We're madly for Adlai. (B 958)
1960--Democratic Party--Kennedy
At the Convention, supporters of Stevenson carried
banners with this slogan.

868. Experience Counts. (B 959)
1960--Republican Party--Nixon
Republicans emphasized Nixon's experience gained
during his Vice-Presidency.

869. They Understand What Peace Demands. (B 959)
1960--Republican Party--Nixon
A slogan in support of Nixon and his running mate,
Henry Cabot Lodge.

870. Get this country moving again. (C 120; BAR 66; S
3464)
    1960--Democratic Party--Kennedy
    A variation of one of Adlai Stevenson's slogans
    (see entry no. 856).

871. A world in which man is the measure of all things.
(J 622)
    1960--Socialist Party

872. Ask not what your country can do for you--ask what
you can do for your country. (MO, v3, 485)
    1961--Kennedy
    From Kennedy's inaugural address.

873. Let us begin. (MO, v3, 485)
    1961--Kennedy
    From Kennedy's inaugural address.

874. Let us continue. (MO, v3, 499)
    1963--Johnson
    A reference to Kennedy's "Let us begin" (see en-
        try no. 873), a phrase in Johnson's first mes-
        sage to Congress.

875. You know where he stands--Vote for the Man You Can
Trust. (LO 879)
    1964--Republican Party--Goldwater

876. The Great Society. (BO 310; L 889; BAR 163; Z 562;
S 3587; LO 869; F 165)
    1964--Democratic Party--Johnson

877. For the people--for a free people. (J 677)
    1964--Republican Party--Goldwater
    From the party platform.

878. A new American greatness. (J 672)
    1964--Democratic Party--Johnson
    From the party platform.

879. America Is One Nation--One People. (J 644; S 3587)
    1964--Democratic Party--Johnson

880. War on Poverty. (BAR 163; C 7; S 3587)
    1964--Democratic Party--Johnson
    One of the elements in Johnson's Great Society.

881. Peace for all Americans. (BAR 182)
        1964--Democratic Party--Johnson
        A slogan soon abrogated by the Vietnam War.

882. Preacher Lyndon. (BAR 172)
        1964--Republican Party--Goldwater
        A nickname for Johnson.

883. Au H$_2$O = 1964. (LO 879)
        1964--Republican Party--Goldwater
        A popular bumper sticker.

884. I have a dream. (Z 448)
        1964--Freedom Democratic Party (Mississippi)
        A slogan derived from Martin Luther King, Jr.'s
          rousing speech in Washington, D.C. in August
          1963.

885. One Man--One Vote. (W 104)
        1964--Freedom Democratic Party
        A slogan of the Student Non-violent Coordinating
          Committee registering black voters in Mississippi.

886. We Shall Overcome. (Z 455; W 106)
        1964--Freedom Democratic Party
        Black delegates from Mississippi demanded to be
          seated instead of the all-white delegation at the
          Atlantic City Convention.

887. All the way with LBJ. (F 161; LO 900)
        1964--Democratic Party--Johnson
        A campaign song and widely used on buttons,
          posters, bumper stickers.

888. Welcome, Doctor Strangewater. (LO 898)
        1964--Democratic Party--Johnson
        A sarcastic attack on Goldwater referring to the
          film Doctor Strangelove.

889. Vote for Goldwater and Go to War. (LO 898)
        1964--Democratic Party--Johnson
        Goldwater was perceived as the aggressive candi-
          date, Johnson the more open to negotiations.

890. If you think, you know he's wrong. (LO 898)
        1964--Democratic Party--Johnson
        Goldwater was depicted as a hardliner who would
          get the United States into a hot war.

891. Goldwater for Hallowe'en.   (C 43; LO 898)
      1964--Democratic Party--Johnson
      Another attack on Goldwater.

892. A party for all Americans.   (S 3588)
      1964--Democratic Party--Johnson
      Vice-Presidential candidate Humphrey used this
         campaign slogan.

893. Crime in the streets.   (LO 897; S 3588)
      1964--Republican Party--Goldwater
      Goldwater attacked the Administration for failure
         to pay attention to this issue.

894. Extremism in the defense of liberty is no vice ...
      and moderation in the pursuit of justice is no virtue.
      (BAR 180; LO 888; L 886)
      1964--Republican Party--Goldwater
      From Goldwater's acceptance speech, then widely
         used as a slogan both for and against him.

895. In Your Heart You Know He's Right.   (BAR 169;
      S 3594)
      1964--Republican Party--Goldwater
      Used extensively on billboards.

896. In your guts you know he's nuts.   (S 3594)
      1964--Democratic Party--Johnson
      An ironic reply to the Goldwater slogan (see en-
         try no. 895).

897. A choice, not an echo.   (LO 870; BAR 181; S 3588)
      1964--Republican Party--Goldwater
      The key slogan of the campaign.

898. We are not going to send American boys nine or ten
      thousand miles away.   (BAR 182)
      1964--Democratic Party--Johnson
      Johnson was campaigning on a promise not to send
         United States military to Vietnam.

899. Peace and Freedom.   (S 3587)
      1964--Democratic Party--Johnson
      Johnson's key campaign issues were civil liberties
         and the war in Vietnam.

900a. Hell, no, we won't go
   b. The whole world is watching

c. Stop the war, stop the war
d. Peace now, peace now
e. Shut the door on the war, we don't want the draft
f. LBJ, LBJ, how many kids did you kill today?
g. Stop the Bombing
h. Fuck you, LBJ. Fuck you, LBJ
   Slogans of the growing opposition to the Vietnam
      War. From chants, banners, leaflets, graffiti,
      etc.

901. The fastest, loosest tongue in the West. (WH 373)
         1968--Republican Party--Nixon
         The Republicans' characterization of Humphrey.

902. This time vote like your whole life depended on it.
      (WH 373)
         1968--Republican Party--Nixon
         From Nixon campaign banners toward the end of
         the campaign.

903. Sir Richard the Chicken-Hearted. (WH 370)
         1968--Democratic Party--Humphrey
         Humphrey's nickname for Nixon because Nixon
         avoided a debate with him.

904. Bomb the Vietnamese back to the Stone Age. (WH
      368)
         1968--American Independent Party--Wallace
         A quote from Curtis LeMay, Vice-Presidential
         candidate.

905. Don't Let Wallace Make This a Police State. (WH
      349)
         1968
         From banners opposing Wallace's candidacy.

906. Hawks and doves. (WH 7)
         1968
         Nicknames for supporters and opponents of the
         Vietnam War.

907. Who can you trust? (W 430)
         1968--Democratic Party--Humphrey
         Humphrey's attack on Nixon during a series of
         speeches.

908. Stand up, stand up, stand up for human rights. (WH
      343)

1968--Democratic Party--Humphrey
From campaign speeches by Humphrey.

909. Mr. Nixon, where do you stand? Where do you
    stand? (WH 342)
        1968--Democratic Party--Humphrey
        Humphrey played on this theme insistently in his
            campaign speeches.

910. Fearless Fosdick. (WH 342)
        1968--Democratic Party--Humphrey
        Humphrey's jeering nickname for Nixon.

911. Dump the Hump. (LO 963)
        1968--Democratic Party--Humphrey
        A slogan at the 1968 Convention by anti-Humphrey
            groups.

912. Sell-Out, Sell-Out. (WH 336)
        1968
        Chants which greeted Humphrey when he gave cam-
            paign speeches after the Democratic Convention.

913. Don't Hump on Me. (WH 336)
        1968
        An anti-Humphrey slogan.

914. Mayor Daley for Heart Donor. (WH 336)
        1968
        Opposition to Mayor Daley of Chicago after the ex-
            plosive Democratic Convention.

915. Cops plus Democrats Equal Pigs. (WH 336)
        1968
        Another slogan showing the anger aroused by the
            "police riot" during the Democratic Convention
            in Chicago.

916. Clean Gene. (WH 326)
        1968
        Eugene McCarthy's nickname during the primary
            campaign.

917. The world won't come to an end if we use a nuclear
    weapon. (S 3747)
        1968--American Independent Party--Wallace
        A quote from Vice-Presidential candidate Curtis
            LeMay.

918. New leadership, new policies. (S 3746)
     1968--Republican Party--Nixon

919. Soft on inflation, soft on communism, soft on law and
     order. (S 3742)
     1968--Republican Party--Nixon
     The Republican attack on the Democrats--from a
     speech by Vice-Presidential candidate Agnew.

920. Bring Us Together. (W 431)
     1968--Republican Party--Nixon

921. Want a Republican President? Nixon's the one.
     (LO 949)
     1968--Republican Party--Nixon

922. End the war and win the peace in the Pacific. (LO
     950)
     1968--Republican Party--Nixon

923. That's the Spirit, Humphrey. (F 183)
     1968--Democratic Party--Humphrey
     A campaign button.

924. The politics of happiness, the politics of purpose, the
     politics of joy. (S 3723; LO 955)
     1968--Democratic Party--Humphrey

925. A government that is responsive and compassionate
     and committed to justice and the rule of law. (J 743)
     1968--Democratic Party--Humphrey
     From the party platform.

926. Think anew and act anew. (J 749)
     1968--Republican Party--Nixon
     From the party platform.

927. The Wallace Way. (F 183)
     1968--American Independent Party--Wallace
     A campaign button.

928. Pointy-headed bureaucrats. (C 20)
     1968--American Independent Party--Wallace

929. The Forgotten Americans. (WH 325)
     1968--Republican Party--Nixon
     Nixon's characterization for the Americans "who

pay taxes, go to church, send their children to school. "

930. Events are in the saddle and ride mankind. (WH 29)
1968--Democratic Party--Humphrey
George Ball began a 1965 memo to Lyndon Johnson with this quote from Ralph Waldo Emerson.
It became a key slogan during the 1968 campaign.

931. Do your own thing. (WH 29)
1968--Democratic Party--Humphrey
A quote from Emerson's "Self Reliance" which became a slogan, especially for black and youth
activists.

932. The way to stop crime is to stop moral decay. (WH
56)
1968--Republican Party--Nixon
Billboards for George Romney during the primaries
used this slogan.

933. Peace with Amnesty. (WH 57)
1968--Republican Party--Nixon
Used by Romney in his Vietnam policy statement
during the primaries.

934. Brainwashing. (WH 59)
1968--Republican Party--Nixon
"I had the greatest brainwashing that anybody can
get when you go over to Vietnam"--a quote from
a TV interview with Romney in 1967 which became a cause célèbre.

935. Hitler is Alive--in the White House. (WH 103)
1968--Democratic Party--Humphrey
An anti-Johnson campaign button.

936. King Lyndon the First. (WH 103)
1968--Democratic Party--Humphrey
A campaign button.

937. End the War and Win the Peace. (WH 130)
1968--Republican Party--Nixon
A pervasive issue during the campaign.

938. Jack was nimble, Jack was quick / But Bobby simply

makes me sick. (WH 151)
1968--Democratic Party--Humphrey
Anti-Robert Kennedy posters during the primaries.

939. We want a Man not a Name. (WH 178)
1968--Democratic Party--Humphrey
An anti-Robert Kennedy placard. He was perceived
as trading on the Kennedy name.

940. Go-Go-Go with Rocky. (WH 234)
1968--Republican Party--Nixon
A slogan during Nelson Rockefeller's brief bid for
the nomination.

941. Rock-Rock-Rock with Rocky. (WH 234)
1968--Republican Party--Nixon
A pro-Rockefeller slogan.

942. Get ready for Kennedy in '68. (WH 281)
1968--Democratic Party--Humphrey
After Robert Kennedy's assassination there was a
flurry of support for Teddy Kennedy's nomination.

943. '72 is too late, '68 is the date. (WH 281)
1968--Democratic Party--Humphrey
A slogan of the draft-Teddy-Kennedy movement.

944. We Want Kennedy. (WH 285)
1968--Democratic Party--Humphrey
Supporters of Teddy Kennedy's nomination used
this slogan.

945. Jobs and Food for All. (WH 277)
1968--Democratic Party--Humphrey
A contingent of the Poor People's Campaign used
this slogan in demonstrations outside the Chicago
Democratic Convention.

946. The Whole World Is Watching. (WH 299)
1968--Democratic Party--Humphrey
A slogan during the Party Convention signifying
disapproval of both the party position on the
Vietnam War and the violence against demon-
strators.

947. We Love Our City, We Love Our Mayor, We Love

Our Police, too. (WH 305)
     1968--Democratic Party--Humphrey
     A slogan used by Chicagoans supporting Mayor
     Daley after violence erupted against demon-
     strators at the Convention.

948. Wallace Remembers the Pueblo. (WH 348)
     1968--American Independent Party--Wallace
     Wallace supporters were still smarting at the
     Pueblo incident in which North Koreans had
     seized the American ship and interrogated the
     captain and the crew.

949. Give America back to the people--Vote Wallace.
     (WH 348)
     1968--American Independent Party--Wallace

950. Wallace--Friend of the Working Man. (WH 348)
     1968--American Independent Party--Wallace
     Some of Wallace's supporters were blue-collar
     Southerners.

951. America--Love It or Leave It. (WH 348)
     1968--American Independent Party--Wallace
     A popular slogan among Wallace supporters, it
     became a widely used slogan on bumper strips,
     billboards, and posters.

952. I worked to buy my house, George. / Protect our
     home. (WH 348)
     1968--American Independent Party--Wallace
     Placards during Wallace speeches.

953. Segregation now, segregation tomorrow and segregation
     forever. (WH 344)
     1968--American Independent Party--Wallace
     A quote from Wallace's inaugural speech as Gov-
     ernor of Alabama in 1963, it continued as a
     theme during his Presidential campaign.

954. Nixon's the One. (F 174)
     1972--Republican Party--Nixon
     Campaign button.

955. Freeze war, not wages, out now. (F 174)
     1972--Democratic Party--McGovern
     Campaign button.

956. Come home, America. (BAR 100; W 431)
   1972--Democratic Party--McGovern
   Appeared on billboards and bumper stickers.

957. Industrial self-government, / Economic democracy.
   (J 889)
   1972--Socialist Labor Party--Jenness

958. New respect for law and order. (J 869)
   1972--Republican Party--Nixon
   From the party platform. "Law and order" became a key slogan in the campaign.

959. War on crime. (J 868)
   1972--Republican Party--Nixon
   From the party platform.

960. A New Partnership. (J 858)
   1972--Republican Party--Nixon
   The partnership was to be between the United
   States and the other "nations of the free world."

961. New Era of Diplomacy. (J 852)
   1972--Republican Party--Nixon
   From the party platform.

962. Reason and order. (J 851)
   1972--Republican Party--Nixon
   From the party platform.

963. A free economy. (J 847)
   1972--Prohibition Party--Munn
   From the party platform.

964. Women's liberation is people liberation. (J 843)
   1972--People's Party--Spock

965. A progressive tax on wealth. (J 830)
   1972--People's Party--Spock

966. Welfare programs for the rich. (J 829)
   1972--People's Party--Spock
   The People's Party's characterization of the Republican and Democratic party platforms.

967. Jobs, Income and Dignity. (J 784)
   1972--Democratic Party--McGovern
   From the party platform.

968. A National Youth Act Administered by Youth for the Needs of Youth. (J 781)
    1972--Communist Party--Hall

969. An End to War, Militarism and Imperialist Intrigue. (J 779)
    1972--Communist Party--Hall

970. Bring All Troops Home Now ! / Stop the Bombing of Indochina! (J 890)
    1972--Socialist Workers Party--Fisher

971. Four More Years. (LO 1002)
    1972--Republican Party--Nixon
    This slogan has regularly surfaced whenever a President has run for re-election.

972. Imperial Presidency. (LO 982)
    1972--Democratic Party--McGovern
    Democrats attacked Nixon's administration as imperialistic and despotic.

973. New Majority. (BAR 103)
    1972--Republican Party--Nixon
    Republicans used this slogan to symbolize their attraction for traditionally Democratic voters.

974. Bring Us Together. (W 431)
    1972--Republican Party--Nixon
    The theme of Nixon's campaign.

975. Stop the bombing! Stop the War! (Z 488)
    1972--Republican Party--Nixon
    Slogan of a group of Vietnam War veterans at the Republican Convention.

976. The little people of America are right. (J 770)
    1972--American Independent Party--Schmitz

977. We are on course in calmer seas with a sure, steady hand at the helm. (J 851)
    1972--Republican Party--Nixon
    From the preamble to the party platform.

978. A better life in a better land in a safer world. (J 851)
    1972--Republican Party--Nixon

979. A position of honor and harmony with all of humanity.
(J 825)
      1972--People's Party--Spock

980. We defend the rights of the individual. (J 820)
      1972--Libertarian Party--Hospers

981. Americans want their country back again. (J 820)
      1972--Democratic Party--McGovern
      From the party platform.

982. Leaders for a change. (F 183)
      1976--Democratic Party--Carter
      From a campaign poster.

983. Vote Dry. (F 183)
      1976--Prohibition Party--Bubar
      A campaign button.

984. You can be sure with Ford. (F 183)
      1976--Republican Party--Ford
      A campaign button.

985. Liberty under law and a just and lasting peace.
(J 986)
      1976--Republican Party--Ford
      From the party platform.

986. A safe and just society. (J 972)
      1976--Republican Party--Ford
      From the party platform.

987. Right to Life. (J 963)
      1976--Prohibition Party--Bubar
      A slogan which became the key theme of the anti-
      abortion New Right.

988. For America's third century, why not the best?
(BO 341; LO 1034; BAR 207; CH 72)
      1976--Democratic Party--Carter
      The title of Carter's book, published in 1974, was
      Why Not the Best?

989. You wouldn't elect your boss as your shop steward. /
Why elect his stooge to public office? (J 915)
      1976--Communist Party--Hall

990. No conflict exists between civil order and individual

rights.   (J 946)
>1976--Libertarian Party--MacBride
>From the party platform.

991. End All Cold War Policies.   (J 915)
>1976--Communist Party--Hall

992. Slash the bloated military budget by 80%.   (J 914)
>1976--Communist Party--Hall

993. I'll never lie to the American people.   (C 7; W 189;
BAR 209; CH 75)
>1976--Democratic Party--Carter
>From a speech to the National Press Club repeated
in many TV campaign spots.

994. The Evangelical's Candidate.   (CH 77)
>1976--Democratic Party--Carter
>From advertisements for Carter in Christian mag-
azines.

995. Born-again Christian.   (CH 77)
>1976--Democratic Party--Carter
>Carter declared himself a "born-again" Christian
as an appeal to the evangelical voters.

996. The Man Who Made Us Proud Again.   (CH 111; BAR
189)
>1976--Republican Party--Ford
>Television commercials for Ford repeated this
theme.

997. Rose Garden strategy.   (CH 94)
>1976--Republican Party--Ford
>Ford stayed in the White House giving television
interviews instead of campaigning across the
country.   Used again about Carter in the 1980
campaign.

998. Outlaw racism.   (J 914)
>1976--Communist Party--Hall

999. Unite against Big Business.   (J 915)
>1976--Communist Party--Hall

1000. Abolish All Anti-Democratic and Repressive Laws.
(J 915)
>1976--Communist Party--Hall

1001.   War Against Inflation.   (W 204)
        1976--Republican Party--Ford

1002.   Giving away the Panama Canal.   (CH 84)
        1980--Republican Party--Reagan
        Republicans accused Carter of having surrendered
            Panama in the 1978 Panama Canal Treaty.

1003.   Reagan for the rich, what about the poor?   (W 396)
        1980--Democratic Party--Carter
        Anti-Reagan sentiment.

1004.   Reagan for Shah.
        1980
        Bumper sticker.

1005.   U. S. Out of North America.
        1980
        Bumper sticker.

1006.   Nobody for President.
        1980
        Bumper sticker.

1007.   If Jimmy Carter Wins, We Lose.   (W 400)
        1980--Republican Party--Reagan

1008.   Bring home our hostages.   (W 396)
        1980--Republican Party--Reagan
        A reference to the American hostages held for
            over a year in Iran.

1009.   Ratify Salt II, End the Arms Race.   (JOH 36)
        1980--Communist Party--Hall

1010.   Fight racism--Defend Democratic Rights.   (JOH 36)
        1980--Communist Party--Hall

1011.   Jobs for All--Stop plant closings.   (JOH 36)
        1980--Communist Party--Hall

1012.   Supply-side economics.   (W 159)
        1980--Republican Party--Reagan
        This slogan, appearing during the campaign, be-
            came a hot issue after the election, a key plank
            in Reagan's economic program, later dubbed
            "Reaganomics."

1013. Economic Recovery Program. (W 204)
       1980--Republican Party--Reagan
       This generalized slogan became "Reaganomics" af-
          ter the election, used proudly by advocates and
          jeeringly by opponents.

1014. The family, the neighborhood, and the workplace.
       (JOH 177)
       1980--Republican Party--Reagan
       Three key issues in the party's platform.

1015. We speak for a patriotism greater than party. (JOH
       176)
       1980--John Anderson
       Anderson ran as an independent candidate.

1016. We must rebuild America. (JOH 102)
       1980--Anderson

1017. We challenge the cult of the omnipotent state and de-
       fend the rights of the individual. (JOH 86)
       1980--Libertarian Party--Clark

1018. The Democratic partnership. (JOH 37)
       1980--Democratic Party--Carter
       From the preamble to the party platform.

1019. Program for the 80's: Humanize America. (JOH
       219)
       1980--Socialist Party--McReynolds

1020. Come, help us build a party of the American peo-
       ple... / Help us shape a more secure future for hu-
       manity. (JOH 20)
       1980--Citizens' Party--Barry Commoner

1021. A Commitment to Economic Fairness. (JOH 38)
       1980--Democratic Party--Carter

1022. Government must ever be the servant of the nation,
       not its master. (JOH 197)
       1980--Republican Party--Reagan
       From the party platform.

1023. With God's help, let us now, together, / make
       America great again. (JOH 177)
       1980--Republican Party--Reagan
       From the preamble to the party platform.

1024.   Beat Reagan--Buy American.   (W 342)
        1980--Democratic Party--Carter

1025.   Reagan--Eat My Grits.   (W 342)
        1980--Democratic Party--Carter
        One of the anti-Reagan slogans that surfaced at
        the Democratic Party Convention.

1026.   Win with Ted.   (W 332)
        1980--Democratic Party--Carter
        Another Convention slogan--from Ted Kennedy
        supporters.

1027.   Four more years, four more years.   (W 332)
        1980--Democratic Party--Carter
        A chant of Carter supporters at the Convention.

1028.   Import peanuts, export Carter.   (W 331)
        1980--Democratic Party--Carter
        A slogan of anti-Carter delegates from New York
        to the Convention.

1029.   Shell that peanut.   (W 326)
        1980--Republican Party--Reagan
        An anti-Carter Convention slogan.   (Carter is a
        peanut farmer.)

1030.   Ron Turns Us On.   (W 326)
        1980--Republican Party--Reagan
        From Reagan supporters at the Republican Party
        Convention.

1031.   Washington State erupts for Reagan.   (W 326)
        1980--Republican Party--Reagan
        A convention slogan referring to the Mount Saint
        Helen's eruption.

1032.   Elephants eat peanuts.   (W 326)
        1980--Republican Party--Reagan
        Anti-Carter sentiments at the Republican Conven-
        tion.

1033.   Life, Liberty and the Pursuit of Reagan.   (W 326)
        1980--Republican Party--Reagan
        Another Convention slogan.

1034.   A noble cause.   (DR 262)

1980--Republican Party--Reagan
Reagan's characterization of the Vietnam War.

1035. Family--Neighborhood--Work--Peace--Freedom.
(DR 266)
1980--Republican Party--Reagan
The persistent themes of the Reagan campaign.

1036. A vote for Anderson is a vote for Reagan. (CH 235)
1980--Democratic Party--Carter
From billboards posted during the campaign.

1037. Moral Majority. (DR 191)
1980--Republican Party--Reagan
Refers to the religious fundamentalist group headed
by evangelist Jerry Falwell; supporters of Reagan's candidacy.

1038. Peace through strength. (DR 211)
1980--Republican Party--Reagan
From a speech by George Bush at the Convention.

1039. The New Right. (DR 190)
1980--Republican Party--Reagan
A coalition around social issues--abortion, busing,
homosexuality, gun control, etc.--whose supporters backed Reagan.

1040. Dumb, dangerous and deceptive. (DR 197)
1980--Republican Party--Reagan
An attack on Carter.

1041. You've got to believe. (CH 175)
1980--Anderson

1042. Reindustrialization of America. (CH 195)
1980--Anderson

1043. ABC Movement--Anybody But Carter. (CH 197)
1980--Democratic Party--Carter
A "dump Carter" slogan at the Democratic Convention.

1044. The time is now for Reagan. (CH 216)
1980--Republican Party--Reagan
From a Republican campaign TV commercial.

1045.   He cares about peace and people.   (CH 219)
        1980--Democratic Party--Carter
        From a TV commercial for Carter.

1046.   People before profits--No Nukes--For a people's
        takeover of the oil industry.   (JOH 227)
        1980--Workers' World Party--Griswold
        The entire platform of the Workers' World Party
        is written in the form of slogans.

1047.   End Sexism; Full rights for gays and lesbians; Pass
        the ERA; For a national gay rights bill.   (JOH 227)
        1980--Workers' World Party--Griswold

1048.   Jobs for all; Stop plant shutdowns; For workers' con-
        trol of industry.   (JOH 227)
        1980--Workers' World Party--Griswold

1049.   Stop the Pentagon's war plans; No draft, no war, no
        way! (JOH 227)
        1980--Workers' World Party--Griswold

1050.   Rebuild the cities; Roll back rents; use Pentagon
        budget for schools, hospitals, housing.   (JOH 227)
        1980--Workers' World Party--Griswold

1051.   End racism and all national oppression; stop police
        brutality; smash the KKK and the Nazis; honor the
        Native treaties; Independence for Puerto Rico.   (JOH
        227)
        1980--Workers' World Party--Griswold

1052.   Defend labor's rights; abolish all anti-labor laws;
        organize the unorganized.   (JOH 227)
        1980--Workers' World Party--Griswold

1053.   Solidarity with workers' struggles abroad.   (JOH 227)
        1980--Workers' World Party--Griswold

1054.   Fight for a system that would end racism, exploita-
        tion, and all forms of oppression; Fight for Social-
        ism! (JOH 227)
        1980--Workers' World Party--Griswold

1055.   Protection for the jobless; End inflation; no "passa-
        longs" to consumers; Eliminate taxes for all income
        under $25,000.
        1980--Workers' World Party--Griswold

1056. Equal opportunity for the disabled, elderly; amnesty
for all undocumented workers. (JOH 227)
1980--Workers' World Party--Griswold

1057. Jobs not jails; Voting rights for all poor and working
people. (JOH 227)
1980--Workers' World Party--Griswold

1058. Voodoo economics. (DR 199; W 305)
1980--Democratic Party--Carter
Originated by Bush during the primaries, then
taken over by the Democrats.

1059. We can turn this country around. (CH 169)
1980--Republican Party--Reagan
A slogan from George Bush, who campaigned for
President during the primaries, then became
Reagan's running mate.

1060. North American Accord. (DR 43)
1980--Republican Party--Reagan
A slogan early in the campaign advocating new re-
lationships between the United States, Canada,
and Mexico.

1061. Together--A New Beginning. (JOH 176; W 431; DR
197)
1980--Republican Party--Reagan
Theme of the Republican Convention Campaign song
by Mike Curb, Lieutenant Governor of California. Included in the preamble of Republican
Party platform.

1062. Reagan and Bush for a New Beginning. (CH 193)
1980--Republican Party--Reagan
The campaign theme from Reagan's acceptance
speech.

KEY TO CITATIONS

Symbol	Author	Title
A	Paul M. Angle	The American Reader
B	Thomas A. Bailey	The American Pageant
BAR	James Barber	The Pulse of Politics
BO	Paul F. Boller, Jr.	Presidential Anecdotes
C	Edward N. Costikyan	How to Win Votes
CCB		A Century of Campaign Buttons
CH	David Chagall	The New King-Makers
DAP		Dictionary of American Politics
DR	Elizabeth Drew	Portrait of an Election
DU	John & Alice Durant	Pictorial History of American Presidents
F	Beryl Frank	Pictorial History of the Democratic Party
H	John D. Hicks	The American Nation
J		National Party Platforms, 1840-1976
JO	Walter Johnson	1600 Pennsylvania Avenue
JOH		National Party Platforms of 1980

L	Arthur S. Link	American Epoch
LO	Stefan Lorant	The Glorious Burden
LOR	Stefan Lorant	The Presidency
M	Ralph G. Martin	Ballots and Bandwagons
MO	Samuel Eliot Morison	The Oxford History of the American People, v. 2 and 3
P	Robert Philippe	Political Graphics
PO	Nelson W. Polsby	Presidential Elections
S	A. M. Schlesinger, Jr.	History of American Presidential Elections, 1789-1968
W	Theodore H. White	America in Search of Itself
WH	Theodore H. White	The Making of the President 1968
Z	Howard Zinn	A People's History of the United States

BIBLIOGRAPHY

Angle, Paul M. The American Reader: From Columbus to Today. New York: Rand McNally and Company, 1958.

Bailey, Thomas A. The American Pageant; A History of the Republic. Boston: D. C. Heath and Company, 2nd ed., 1961.

Barber, James. The Pulse of Politics; Electing Presidents in the Media Age. New York: Norton, 1980.

Boller, Paul F., Jr. Presidential Anecdotes. New York: Oxford University Press, 1981.

A Century of Campaign Buttons, 1789-1889. Compiled by J. Doyle DeWitt. Hartford, Conn.: J. Doyle DeWitt, 1959.

Chagall, David. The New King-makers. New York: Harcourt Brace Jovanovich, 1981.

Costikyan, Edward N. How to Win Voters: The Politics of 1980. New York: Harcourt Brace Jovanovich, 1980.

Dictionary of American Politics. Edited by Edward Conrad Smith and Arnold John Zurcher. New York: Barnes and Noble, Inc., 1961.

Drew, Elizabeth. Portrait of an Election: The 1980 Presidential Campaign. New York: Simon and Schuster, 1981.

117

Durant, John and Alice. Pictorial History of American Presidents. New York: A. S. Barnes and Company, 1956.

Frank, Beryl. Pictorial History of the Democratic Party. Secaucus, N.J.: Castle Books, 1980.

Hicks, John D. The American Nation, A History of the United States from 1865 to the Present. Boston: Houghton Mifflin Company, 1945.

Johnson, Walter. 1600 Pennsylvania Avenue: Presidents and the People, 1929-1959. Boston: Little, Brown and Company, 1960.

Link, Arthur S. American Epoch: A History of the United States Since the 1890's. New York: Alfred A. Knopf, 3rd ed., 1967.

Lorant, Stefan. The Glorious Burden: The History of the Presidency from George Washington to James Earl Carter, Jr. Lenox, Mass.: Author's Edition, Inc., 1976.

_____. The Presidency: A Pictorial History of Presidential Elections from Washington to Truman. New York: Macmillan Co., 1953.

Martin, Ralph G. Ballots & Bandwagons. Chicago: Rand McNally & Company, 1964.

Morison, Samuel Eliot. The Oxford History of the American People. 3 vols. New York: New American Library, 1972.

National Party Platforms. Compiled by Donald Bruce Johnson. Vol. I: 1840-1956 ; Vol. II: 1960-1976. Urbana, Ill.: University of Illinois Press, 1978.

National Party Platforms of 1980. Compiled by Donald Bruce Johnson. Urbana, Ill.: University of Illinois Press, 1982.

Philippe, Robert. Political Graphics: Art as a Weapon. New York: Abbeville Press, 1982.

Polsby, Nelson W. Presidential Elections: Strategies of American Electoral Politics. New York: Scribners, 1980.

Schlesinger, Arthur M., Jr. History of American Presidential Elections, 1789-1968. 4 vols. New York: Chelsea House Publishers, in association with McGraw-Hill Co., 1971.

White, Theodore H. America in Search of Itself; The Making of the President, 1956-1980. New York: Harper & Row, 1982.

_____. The Making of the President 1968. New York: Atheneum Publishers, 1969.

Zinn, Howard. A People's History of the United States. New York: Harper & Row, 1980.

Abolitionists see Liberty Party

Christian Nationalist Party (1948) 809
Citizens Party (1980) 1020
Communist Party (1932-) 682-683, 698, 710, 712, 718-
    721, 746, 763-766, 780, 968-969, 989, 991-992, 998-
    1000, 1009-1011
Constitutional Union Party (1860) 239, 247

Democratic Party (1824-) 34, 36, 38, 40-41, 43-46, 48,
    50-56, 58-59, 61, 64-66, 72, 75-78, 81-83, 85-90, 92-
    93, 95, 98, 101-105, 112, 114, 116-122, 141, 144-145,
    147-153, 160, 163, 175-181, 187-188, 193-195, 198,
    200-202, 204, 208-209, 214, 224-225, 228, 233, 251-
    253, 264, 270, 274-276, 278-279, 283, 289, 294-295,
    297-301, 305, 308-311, 314-315, 318, 326, 337-342,
    345, 347-352, 356, 360, 365, 368, 370-372, 374, 376-
    381, 387-389, 391-392, 398, 403, 406, 408, 410-412,
    417-419, 421-423, 428-433, 437, 445, 452, 456-457,
    460, 464, 468, 470, 475, 480-481, 483, 485-489, 491-
    492, 495, 503, 506, 509, 513-515, 520, 525, 530, 534,
    536-539, 543, 545, 547, 556, 559, 560, 564, 567, 580,
    582, 584-587, 589, 593-597, 609-610, 612, 618, 623,
    625-626, 632, 635, 637, 640, 642, 646-647, 657-676,
    679-680, 694-697, 701, 704-705, 708, 713, 732, 734,
    736-737, 739, 741-744, 750-751, 759, 776-779, 782-
    783, 790, 795-796, 800, 802, 804, 806, 808, 810, 814,
    820, 823, 844-845, 848, 850, 854-856, 858-862, 865,

125

Class, Working Men 171, 399, 532, 604d, 628, 650, 710, 761, 950, 952, 1035, 1048, 1053, 1056-1057

Worst 678

Wrong 890

Yankees, Yanks 41, 604i, 772b

Years 460, 552, 701, 840, 971, 1027

Yellow-bellied 773b

Yellow Peril 404, 543

Youth 968